Turn & jump: how time & place fell
304.2 MAN
P9-DNU-899
Libbie Cass Library

DISCARD

Libbie A. Cass Library
PO Box 89
Springfield, NH 03284
763-4381 spfldlibrary@emiot.com

TURN & JUMP

Books by Howard Mansfield

Cosmopolis
In the Memory House
Skylark
The Same Ax, Twice
The Bones of the Earth

Editor
Where the Mountain Stands Alone

For Children
Hogwood Steps Out

Howard Mansfield

Copyright © 2010 by Howard Mansfield
All rights reserved.

ISBN 978-0-89272-816-9

Design by Lynda Chilton
Cover photograph by Emily Lilienthal

Printed in the United States of America
5 4 3 2 1

Distributed to the trade by National Book Network

Library of Congress Cataloging-in-Publication Data

Mansfield, Howard.
Turn and jump : how time and place fell apart / Howard Mansfield.
p. cm.
Includes bibliographical references.
ISBN 978-0-89272-816-9 (hardcover : alk. paper)
1. Time--Social aspects. 2. Time perception. 3. Clocks and watches. I. Title.
HM656.M25 2010
304.2'37--dc22
2010005264

Once again for
Dr. B. A. Millmoss

“Time, just as it is, is being, and being is all time.”

—Zen Master Eihei Dogen (1200–1253)

“All the old rhythm is gone and in its place is heard the hum of an engine, the whirr of wheels, the explosion of an exhaust. The leisurely songs that men hummed to the clatter of horses’ hoofs do not fit into this new rhythm. . . . The new age demands new music for new action.”

—Master Songwriter Irving Berlin, 1924

Contents

Introduction
Clock. Clock. Clock.

On an October morning, when the air and light were like a tonic, I sat in a museum of stilled machines and old filed papers, the only visitor. I sat at a desk between two clocks. A grandfather clock was behind me and an office regulator clock, with a large pendulum, was in front. The clocks ticked loudly; they ticked in unison. *Clock-clock-clock.* I could feel the pendulums swing in my gut. Everything else in the museum was mute—the Model A, the steam-engine pumper, the children's toy metal cars. The clocks were insistent. Time was ticking through me.

I have been to this small museum several times. Each time I am the only visitor and each time I am welcomed by an elderly volunteer happy for the company. On this visit, a woman, who had lost some portion of her sight, insisted on showing me around. She wanted to be of help, but when I asked her for the files in "Drawer E," she had no idea that they had a Drawer E, or where it might be, or even where to find the pencil sharpener. She went off to call someone who might know. I was alone with the clocks.

Out the window I could see the electric current of October light.

Clock-clock-clock.

On my next visit, an elderly gentleman met me. He knew where Drawer E was, but before he took me to it, he insisted on telling me a long story, the story of his life. He began when his ancestors came to town in the 1880s from a neighboring town, and he took me through various summer jobs spent haying and roofing, followed by college (only the fourth person from his town to go), then World War II (32 months in the Pacific without firing a shot—he'd seen more action on the Fourth of July), and home to a long career with one company in some kind of engineering and management. He fixed his gaze on me. The clocks ticked. Though I was anxious to finally read what was in Drawer E, I followed his story and asked questions. He was presenting me with another clock.

We now had at least four clocks in the room: his clock (*how-it-was, how-it-was*), my clock (*can-we-get-going*?), and the two antiques clocking away. If he ever did bring me the files, there would be another clock in the room. Every historical event moves to its own time, and if you pay close attention, you may catch its cadence—in a phrase in a letter, in the poise of the handwriting, or in the way one letter answers another. What we want from the past is presence. We want the moment restored. We want the October day that I could see out the window: a row of old maples shimmering yellow-gold. A blue sky. The sound now and then of children at recess, mobbing a soccer ball.

I finally did read the papers in Drawer E. When I drove away, I could still hear those two clocks. I have thought about the clocks for years. Why did this bother me? I have heard these clocks in other places. I have heard them in the ordinary sentences of local histories, sentences like: "Josiah Prescott arrived in 1798, cleared sixty acres, married Ann Cummings who died in childbirth leaving nine children, four of whom were lost to the epidemic the following year. Prescott abandoned the homestead, which eventually burned, went west, remarried, and was never heard from again."

This kind of two-sentence biography is common in local histories. These sentences swim by in schools, each sentence a lifetime of suffering and struggle. Mortality: Another clock ticking.

Clock-clock-clock. The clocks were like a heartbeat, that's why I found them so disturbing. We are all clocks. We are time, says Zen Master Dogen. "Time, just as it is, is being, and being is all time."

Jorge Luis Borges says, "Time is the substance I am made of. Time is a river which sweeps me along, but I am the river; it is a tiger which destroys me, but I am the tiger; it is a fire which consumes me, but I am the fire." This is what I heard in the old clocks. It's why I first began to think about this book.

My previous books have searched for ways to see the deep time hidden in the common place. *In the Memory House* looked at the way we create our history. Each chapter explored how we choose our ancestors, choose who gets to enter the memory house—whose names are on the landscape, monuments, and holidays. *The Same Ax, Twice* pursued a living past, a past that gives us the vision to shape the future. I was searching for a past that wasn't stop-time, wasn't a frozen museum. My last book, *The Bones of the Earth*, looked at the way people still carry the allegiances to the oldest landmarks—sticks and stones.

This is a book about time and place. They were once inseparable. Science historians note that before Thomas Edison, light and fire were the same thing; after Edison they were separate. The same can be said of time and place. Before the railroads created Standard Time zones in 1883, and international time zones were adopted the next year, time and place were one. After this, time was divorced from the rising of the sun—off four minutes in one place, 18 or 36 minutes in another place. Time became a uniform commodity. Local time is "a relic of antiquity," said the director of an astronomical observatory that sold time to subscribers, just as the utilities sold gas or water. Go down the long roster of 19th-century inventions, and you can check off the many inventions that wrested local time from its throne—the railroad, the telegraph, the limited-liability corporation, to name just three.

Timekeeping changed in two important ways in the late 19th and early 20th centuries—clocks became more accurate and were linked to each other. Time reformers spoke of linking all clocks on earth to one master clock. But at the same moment, time escaped out the front door. "There are many clocks," said Einstein in 1905. "There is no time, but times," said his teacher, the physicist Hermann Minkowski in 1908. "Space and time are in the eye of the beholder. Each of us carries our own clock, our own monitor of the passage of time," physicist Brian Greene writes in *The Fabric of the Cosmos.*

This book is a look at some of the clocks we carry. I look at time in the invention of Continuous Vaudeville; in a once-common, now-vanished dry-goods shop; in an old mill family defending water-power rights; in a Broadway hit of the 1880s that is still performed annually on an outdoor stage; and in the lingering effects of a bloody war that one historian calls the first American Revolution, a war many Americans don't even know happened. As in my other books, most of the stories come from the New Hampshire land in sight of Mount Monadnock. After twenty-five years, this place is still teaching me to see.

This book's title—*Turn & Jump*—is taken from the pioneers who helped to build a national culture: variety and vaudeville actors. For their "turn" on stage they traveled long distances, spending days and nights on trains making the "jump." Turn and jump. Slapstick and knockabout. The language has the feel of rough travel over badly maintained railroad track. Business travelers live this life today. Turn and jump: it's the cadence of many lives.

Each chapter moves to its own clock. In each essay we take the measure of a different time flow. "No single clock can in itself measure time. It is always necessary to compare at least two clock-like processes," writes philosopher J. T. Fraser, in *Time, The Familiar Stranger.* I'm looking for levels of time, different clocks that I can set running and then compare, metaphors with which to unlock the ordinary.

The longer chapters are introduced by short "Timescape" chapters. Each Timescape sets up the theme of the next chapter. Timescapes are landscapes of time—the tempo and duration that live in a place. "Just as we can survey space as a landscape spread before us, so we can survey time (in our mind's eye at least) as a *timescape* timelessly laid out," Paul Davies writes in *About Time.* I apply this idea to get away from the past-present-future timeline and to regard "time," as Davies writes, "like space, as simply there."

Turn & Jump explores the divorce of time and place, of timekeeping from the way we dwell in and tend the places we call home.

Many years after I had sat between those two insistent clocks, I learned that my unease was one that folklorists had also noted. When people began to live with clocks in their homes, a body of popular belief and superstition grew up to domesticate the strangeness. It was considered bad luck to have two clocks ticking in the same room, or the same house. "My grandmother would not do that for anything, for she said it was sure death," one folklorist was told.

One clock in your house changed things, changed the way the day itself was lived, but two clocks (almost certain to disagree) could call into question the authority of this machine, or even mock God, the master clockmaker. Two clocks, sounding noon minutes apart, speak too plainly the truth that clocks are a fiction we accept in order to get on with our day. In the time between two noons in one living room, there is the space for doubt to enter. It allows the truth to come calling: We don't know what time is, but we know that our allotment is limited.

We domesticate time the best that we can. It's why we do not understand the physicists when they throw out *past-present-future*, and why no matter how many times they explain that time slows down as you approach the speed of light, we walk away still married to a notion of absolute time, steady time, from Newton's lips to God's ears. It's been a hundred years since Einstein began to shake things up, but still we live as if Newton had gotten in the last word on the apple falling from the tree. In our time-ignorance, we are adherents of the flat earth. But there is no one absolute time. We live in many times, with many clocks. We are ourselves many clocks—biological rhythms upon rhythms.

Once I saw a great clock in an old family home. The family had lived for several generations in a grand Federal-style house built in 1821 on a New England common. They were one of those outstanding families whose house, with its casual grace, makes you think they are on a first-name basis with time, and that while they haven't cheated mortality, they've done some trick with mirrors and portraits and memoirs that has stretched time—as if one of their years is equal to seven of ours.

The house had an elegant entrance, a central hall with a stairway spiraling up three stories. The cherry handrail was satin to the touch. In the entry stood an antique grandfather clock. The works were missing. The hands were missing. The inside of the clock, where the pendulum would have been, was filled with mittens and gloves, layers of red wool and black leather, of blue, white, and green, going back winters upon winters. It was like a geological deposit, like snowfall. There were children's mittens deep in the pile that once belonged to boys and girls who were grandparents now. This is a measure of time we can understand. Tell us how many mittens it has been since then, how many gloves since the winter the blizzard shut everything down for days. This was a clock within a clock, with the minutes and hours silenced and the generations ticking away. There is always more than one clock in the room.

Timescape:
"Did But Little. Caught One Shad."

Esq. Stiles can remember when (1786, or thereabout) there were but four time-pieces in town. These were old-fashioned box-clocks, which, together with the chimney, took up no small part of a house in those days, reports *The History of Temple, New Hampshire* (1860). "Most people used the hour-glass. . . . Some people used sun-dials, and all had their 'noon-marks.'" The hour and the minute were not important. Time was kept in other ways, marked in the terse entries of farmers' diaries:

April ye 4th 1803. Fair; began ploughing in earnest; sowed peas.

April ye 8th 1803. Cloudy; raw and chilly wind from S.E. to S.W. alternately; small rain at evening; sowed 1 bushel of rye & ½ bushel of wheat. Set cabbage stumps . . .

April ye 22d 1803. Fair & pleasant wind [from] N.W. Augustus fortunate in catching trouts.

April ye 27th 1803. Cloudy & chilly wind N.E. Sowed 12 qts F. seed & peas and turnip seed.

April ye 29th 1803. Planted 4 Bush of Potatoes.

May ye 17th 1803. Warm & pleasant, wind W. Did but little. Caught 1 shad.

This is Ebenezer Edwards' diary. Edwards was a representative man of the early period, coming to Temple in 1780. Originally from Acton, Massachusetts, he had served with the Acton Company of Minute Men at Concord Bridge in April 1775. Edwards represented Temple in the state legislature for fourteen years, and was a "fluent and dignified" town meeting moderator for twenty years. He ran a store and built a "pearl ashery." Pearl ash, a refined potash (which is made from wood ash), was used for making soap. "Trade was carried on upon credit altogether. The store-keeper collected all the country produce and sent it to market by ox-teams; sometimes five or six ox-teams filed along the road," says the Temple history. "The main articles were butter, '3 or 4 tons potash, and 3000 or 4000 yards tow cloth.'" The Temple of Edwards' era, a town of some 850 people, included these enterprises: carpenters, plough makers, blacksmiths, millers, cider makers, maple-sugar makers, tanners, and shoemakers. ("If you wanted a pair of shoes . . . you would get your leather at the tanner's and carry it to the shoemaker.") By 1817, Temple had four grain mills, three sawmills, and one fulling mill.

Edwards' diary was a companion to the almanac, the most popular book in America after the Bible. (The second book published in America was an almanac.) Almanacs—"timetables of the skies"—were household necessities. With their tables of sunrise and sunset, almanacs were the indispensable clocks of their day. Calendars, either on the wall or the desk, were not common until after the Civil War. Diaries were sometimes kept in almanacs, amendments to note local conditions. Some almanacs provided empty pages for notes. (It is not known how Edwards kept his diary.)

In Edward's diary the chief unit of time is the season. It is a local almanac:

May ye 26th 1803. Fair & warm; wind S.E. planted squashes, cucumbers, water-melons and muskmelons.

June ye 29th 1803. Finished hoeing corn ye 2d time.

July ye 4th 1803. Fair & pleasant; wind N. Began haying in earnest.

July ye 10th 1803. Sunday, fair & warm; wind W. Dined on green peas. Mr. Farrar preached with us.

Aug. ye 2d 1803. Fair and warm; wind N.W. put in 2 Load Rye.

Aug. ye 14th 1803. Had roasted corn.

Sept. ye 12th 1803. Fair & pleasant; wind E. Gathered onions & beans & began to dig potatoes.

Oct. ye 21st 1803. Fair and pleasant. Wind W. Finished gathering apples.

The sun was the chief clock, but the moon was also a watched clock. Almanacs had tables for "The Rising, Setting and Southing of the moon;" tables listing the lunar influence on "head, neck, arms, breast, heart, belly, reins [ribs], secrets, thighs, knees, legs, feet;" and advice to plan your work by the phases of the moon. ("On the 15th day of the moon, you must begin no work; it is a grievous day.") Edwards, too, followed some of this practical astrology:

April ye 20th 1803: Cut pine timber for shingles & left one log to see if ye worms will injure it: it being the day before the moon changes.

July ye 26 1803: Cut two pine trees precisely on the 1st quarter of the moon.

Almanacs and the importance of being weatherwise kept farmers attuned to time, but it was time as set by the sun, moon, and stars, not set by other clocks. Noon time is unvarying by the clock, but it changes daily if you read the shadows cast by a "noon mark." This was strictly local time—the time of this place, the time to plant in this particular field. By the standards of his era, Edwards was on time. He attended to the seasons; he worked hard. In New England, the work ethic and religious injunctions against idleness were in place long before clocks were common. In 1633 Massachusetts Puritans passed a law against time-wasting: "No person, householder, or other shall spend his time idly or unprofitably, under the pain of such punishment as the court shall think meet to inflict." Time belonged to God and wasting it was an offense. This was a culture that believed in "improving the time." English Puritan Ralph Thoresby invented the alarm clock. Boston-born Benjamin Franklin ("time is money") invented Daylight Saving Time in an effort to reform slothful, late-rising Parisians.

Lucy Larcom, a Lowell mill girl born in 1824, recalled a Massachusetts childhood "penetrated through every fiber of thought with the idea that idleness is a disgrace. It was taught with the alphabet and the spelling book; it was enforced by precept and example, at home and abroad; and it is to be confessed that it did sometimes haunt the childish imagination almost mercilessly." Some schools had a clock in each classroom by the 1830s. "Time discipline" was also taught to "civilize" Indian children and to "Americanize" immigrants.

Improvements in timekeeping were encouraged. The first colonists imported expensive clocks. By 1830 more than a hundred workshops in Connecticut were mass-producing cheaper, more democratic models with wooden gears. These clocks were sold by peddlers throughout the countryside on sales routes that lasted months. Travelers found Connecticut clocks on the frontier. "Wherever we have been, in Kentucky, in Indiana, in Illinois, in Missouri, and here in every dell of Arkansas, and in cabins where there was not a chair to sit on, there was sure to be a Connecticut clock," reported an English visitor in 1844.

Throughout the 19th century a more uniform clock time began to take hold. "Nature" and "time" had meant the same thing, says historian Michael O'Malley. But "by the 1830s a sense of time rooted in nature confronted a seemingly arbitrary time based in commerce, revealing itself in machine movements and the linear progress of invention." At first only a few businessmen and postmen required accurate time. The federal government built post roads and in 1796 published a popular map showing an hour-by-hour schedule of the north-south postal route—Maine to South

Carolina. Postmasters enforced the schedule on mail riders and coaches. In the 1790s, a letter took forty days to travel from Portland, Maine, to Savannah, Georgia; by 1810 this had been shaved to 27 days. Edwards' small New Hampshire town was fortunate to have regular service on a local postal circuit—the post rider came through every two weeks.

The tempo of commerce quickened. The average Colonial American merchant in a thriving port spent only three hours a day on business, leaving many hours free to spend in the tavern or at church. A busy merchant, trading overseas, might handle about thirty transactions a day, dispatch four to six letters a week, and receive two or three letters. It took four months to exchange letters between Boston and London. Sailing ships crossed the Atlantic only when fully loaded and in good weather. A three-month layover in port was common; it could take a month just to load a ship. There were almost no crossings in January and February, but starting in 1818 regularly scheduled packet lines reduced the crossing time. As factories increased in size, more people went on the clock, paid by the hour, not the day. Ebenezer Edwards' village world of almanacs, hourglasses, "noon marks," and a few clocks was rapidly receding.

Americans in Edwards' day regarded watches and clocks "as mere representations or symbols of time, not as the embodiment of time itself," writes O'Malley. When they had clocks, each town, each farm, set them to follow the transit of the sun. Each spot on earth had its own local time. "But in the act of telling time the clock tended to become the thing it represented—clocks became not imitations or transcripts of time, but time itself."

Two generations after farmer Edwards, Ralph Waldo Emerson wrote in 1841, "The civilized man . . . has a fine Geneva watch but he fails of the skill to tell the hour by the sun . . . the man in the street does not know a star in the sky. The solstice he does not observe; the equinox he knows as little; and the whole bright calendar of the year is without a dial in his mind."

America was a crucible waiting for accurate clocks and organized schedules.

The Continuous

I. Striking the Endless Match

Benjamin Franklin Keith was an orphaned New England farm boy trying to make his way in the world. In his first boyhood money-making ventures he drove cows to pasture (six cents a week) and caught rats for a neighbor (a penny each). Starting out on his own just after the Civil War, he peddled pictures of Abraham Lincoln, clerked in a grocery store, worked as a mess boy on a freighter, lost money making and selling brooms, traveled with several circuses, ran a freak show, and sold "endless" matches. He would go on to combine the last two schemes to create something new.

On the day before Thanksgiving 1869, Keith was hired on the *Ashland*, a freight steamer working the coast from New York City to New Orleans. He had put to sea for the promise of a Thanksgiving dinner. "I had no where else to find it," he said. He was paid $25 a month. "But it was a shame to take the money, even in so small an amount for I was perfectly useless on board when the waves commenced to roll. I persevered, however, for one whole year, after suffering more than I ever wish to again, in that kind of way." He learned to "shift for himself." "In those days I would not have been afraid to be set down empty handed in any quarter of the world where I could speak the language," he recalled. "I felt sure of the ability to produce in some kind of industrial way."

Back on land he started in business, buying a job lot of the "endless match." "This was a match which would furnish 10,000 lights for your cigar provided you were fortunate enough to be able to light it at all. While it was generally possible to light it, occasionally it failed. This caused a decrease in its original popularity, so that I was able to buy up the remnant at job lot prices." Rather than rent a store, he "took possession of any stretch of sidewalk that seemed promising by right of eminent wandering domain and attracted the multitude by continually 'striking a light.' I became so expert at this as to be able to challenge the ability of the famous 'Irishman who can always light his pipe in a gale of wind.'" He sold all his matches, at half their original price, made a "good profit" and moved on.

"I was at Wabash, Indiana, and had negotiated for the privilege of selling my wares during the week on the Fair Ground by paying the sum of one dollar for the entire week, when along came the famous Bachelder and Doris Show consisting of an aviary, caravan, hippodrome and Quinquplexical circus. What that lengthy word may mean I have never been able to ascertain," he said, but he was smitten. "When I got with the circus and heard the band play I felt that I had reached the Elysium Fields where there could be no more sorrow and care." He left with the circus, and traveled an entire season with it. He traveled with other circuses, including Barnum's. Keith did not say what he did for the circus, but he was likely a grifter, a word applied to those who ran the sideshows and to swindlers. Usually the two went together. Circuses and carnivals lived by short-changing the locals. Keith, by character, was more of a hustler than a swindler, someone with a talent for picking your pocket by getting you to buy something that might be less than promised. He looked like the kind of proper dry-goods merchant found in any town. His studio photo shows a respectable bald man with a full mustache. He worked twelve hours a day for the circus and for himself, buying and selling retail and wholesale goods. "There really were no days that I did not enjoy," he said.

The circus was a great school, offering "more practical education for a limited period than the better average of other fields of labor, recreation and enjoyment combined. . . . One possessing a grain of ambition cannot fail to learn much that is of the greatest value in after years, and many will be inclined to add, much that is injurious."

At age 37 he moved to Boston to start his own show. He had been on the road, on trains and horse-drawn wagons, and at sea, for more than twenty years. With a partner he opened a museum—the high-toned name fronted by variety shows—with one attraction, "Baby Alice: The Midget Wonder." Baby Alice, a premature black baby, weighed one and a half pounds. As cruel as this seems today, such "freak" attractions were common. Business was light, so he added the "Circassian Lady" and the "Three-Headed Songstress"—one woman and many mirrors that took up the six-foot square stage. The "Tattooed Man" and "Dog-Faced Boy" followed, and Keith began to prosper. He and a partner opened a new theater, an ornate (and reputedly fireproof) fantasy with a large "ormolu" chandelier "made for the Khedive of Egypt" hanging from the center of a "Moorish" dome.

From one show to the next, Keith struggled to fill the new theater. "I was at my wits end what to do in order to have the appearance of success or in other words, to always have an audience."

Each day, each hour, a showman faces one challenge: Get people in the seats. Keith had been schooled in the ballyhoo of the circus and of sidewalk sales. What draws people? Other people. Crowds attract crowds. This is why a hot Broadway show will prolong the wait at the box office. They want long lines in front of the theater. This is the mob mentality that inflates stock market bubbles and propels bestselling books. Popularity builds on itself.

"In the days of my first shows," Keith said, "I was always maneuvering to keep patrons moving up and down stairs in view of passersby on the sidewalk for the specific purpose of impressing them with the idea that business was immense." Keith's motto, said one employee, was "get the coin."

An empty theater was "dreary" and it was hard to get people in for the next show. In "a sort of half dream between waking and sleeping" Keith found the way to fill seats: Don't let the audience leave. Keep them as bait, as the seed for the next crop. Run the show continuously. "Did you ever notice the hesitancy on the part of early comers to a playhouse to assume their seats in the auditorium, how they hang back until reassured by numbers?" he asked. "Well, that is one of the things the continuous performance does away with. It matters not at what hour of the day or evening you visit, the theater is always occupied by more or less people, the show is in full swing, everything is bright, cheerful and inviting." He improvised and sent out one act for the second time, a lecturer on the tragic Greely Expedition. The act's sole prop was "The Arctic Moon," a handmade newspaper composed by a member of the expedition who had starved to death.

The lecturer was reluctant. "Really, Mr. Keith, it's no use to go out there; they are all the same people and have been here for two hours now, but of course I will go if you say so," he said.

"I'd rather you would," Keith replied. The act went on "and that was the beginning of the second show of the 'continuous.'" Keith later framed that small newspaper and hung it in his office.

Continuous Vaudeville was born. It was like the endless match. Keith just had to strike a light once—attract that initial audience—and he could keep his theater going.

The Continuous ran for twelve hours. The better acts appeared twice, and the lesser acts three times. For ten cents you could sit there all day, but only about two percent of the audience did. The management expected to sell out the house two-and-a-half times a day, and four times on holidays.

Keith wanted the audience to stay, but not all of it, so he sent out a "chaser." Lecturers like the one on the Arctic Moon were usually chasers. The chaser was a turnover specialist, an act poised between attraction and repulsion. He had to be good enough to be entertaining once, but not so entertaining that the audience wanted to see him again. Some vaudeville artists spent their entire careers knowing that they were there to perform to the accompaniment of seats snapping closed and people trooping up the aisles. Loew's American Music Hall employed an act so adept at chasing away customers they had the poor man running between their main theater and their rooftop garden theater. He did impressions in clay, modeling famous faces. He was an "inept" sculptor, but "he never had to worry about being laid off because he was the best chaser in vaudeville." (Only at Sing Sing, doing a Christmas show, did the chasers fail, for obvious reasons. The inmates called the chasers back for encores.)

A competing showman beat Keith to New York City with Continuous Vaudeville. Like Keith, F. F. Proctor was a New England farm boy who had left home in his youth. Proctor was nine when his father died and his mother moved her children back to her family's farm. Starting out, the young Proctor worked as a dry-goods clerk. On his lunch hour he practiced acrobatics on a trapeze in the store's basement. He created a successful vaudeville "equilibrist" act and toured for years before buying his first theater. In 1892 he converted his New York theater from two shows a day to a continuous performance in order to attract the women in the Ladies' Mile department stores. He offered "Ladies Club Theatre," twenty acts from 11 a.m. to 11 p.m., advertising in "every shop window, trolley car, hotel news-stand, every elevated train" in the city. "One of his greatest advertising slogans at this time," says a biography, "impressed upon the public the meaning of continuous:"

After Breakfast Go To Proctor's
After Proctor's Go To Bed

He found ingenious ways to get his message heard. "Mr. Proctor's press agent trained two hundred or more parrots to repeat the words, 'After Breakfast Go To Proctor's.' These birds were offered as prizes to all holders of green admission tickets." Another ad defined the novel idea of "the continuous" this way: "Come At Any Time. Remain As Long As You Please. . . . Always Crowded."

Some mothers found Proctor's "home of perpetual entertainment" wholesome enough to use as a daycare center, sending their children off in the morning with lunch and even supper. "Mothers would sometimes come to the manager and say, 'Will you please help me find my children in your theater? I know they're here, for I sent them here after breakfast and told them to stay all day. It's safer for them in the theater than in the street.'" The manager would make an announcement from the stage.

The public took to Continuous Vaudeville. By 1901 the Continuous was a familiar term; in newspapers it no longer appeared inside quotes. Proctor continually updated the Continuous, "interlarding" short plays with vaudeville acts, and later staging a three-hour program consisting of a short play, vaudeville, and a circus show.

The Continuous was the making of vaudeville. Keith, credited with first applying the word *vaudeville* to variety shows, was a founder of the vaudeville era that thrived from the 1890s to the 1920s. Keith became a millionaire, one of the first ever in show business.

Keith's one theater in Boston drew 40,000 people each week, about 14 percent of the city's population in 1900. This is a conservative estimate by a theater historian who figures the house at only 65 percent of capacity, which the major vaudeville circuits regarded as a profitable operation. With his partner, E. F. Albee, Keith built a circuit of lavish theaters and dominated big-time vaudeville with a monopoly booking acts.

Keith and Albee cleaned up the old variety shows, creating middle-class entertainment. Variety shows were vulgar, performed in smoky beer halls or dives for working-class men. Vaudeville took the acts out of the saloons and made them respectable for women and children to see in attractive theaters. A 1910 survey showed that women made up one-third of New York's vaudeville audience. In San Francisco,

Milwaukee, and other cities, women and children were nearly half the audience. Vaudeville was a New England reform.

Keith's New Theatre opened in Boston in 1894. It was a "dream palace" with marble, mirrors, large paintings, leather-and-brass sofas, swinging doors upholstered in leather and trimmed with silver plates, "elegant vases and jardinières," and a gilded proscenium arch. In the boiler room, the coal came down a polished brass chute. The coal was shoveled into the furnace by firemen in white uniforms. (On request they used "solid silver" shovels.) The furnace room had a red velvet rug, marble-topped tables, and potted plants. It was a good show; it was good press. It advertised Albee's motto: "Cleanliness, Comfort, and Courtesy." People came from afar to see the furnace room and the marble switchboard for the theater's electric system.

The elaborate Boston theaters were reportedly financed by the Catholic church. Performances were monitored by the superintendent of one of Boston's biggest Sunday schools. (If you're going to be idle, at least don't be profane.) Performers called Keith's "the Sunday School circuit."

Every Keith theater reviewed and censored all acts. "I must know exactly what every performer on my stage would say or do. If there was one coarse, vulgar, or suggestive line or piece of business in the act, I cut it out," said Keith. He banned material that would offend "the Irishman, the Jew, or the Down East Yank like myself." He banned mother-in-law jokes and streetcar conductor jokes. Long after he had stopped managing his theaters, there was a regular column in Variety called "You Mustn't Say That." Forbidden in 1921: songs with the words "hot dog," "that's the cat's meow," "the cat's pajamas," and "hot cat." Backstage was posted:

NOTICE TO PERFORMERS

You are hereby warned that your act must be free from all vulgarity and suggestiveness in words, action, and costume

> . . . all vulgar, double-meaning and profane words and songs must be cut out of your act before the first performance. . . .
>
> Such words as Liar, Slob, Son-of-A-Gun, Devil, Sucker, Damn, and all others unfit for the ears of ladies and children, also any references to questionable streets, resorts, localities, and barrooms, are prohibited under fine of instant discharge.
>
> GENERAL MANAGER

Just as Keith taught his actors to behave, he taught his audiences to behave. At the first performance in his Providence house he came on stage to quiet the rowdy "gallery gods" who hissed, cat-called, and clapped in unison to shut down an act. "You can't do that here," he announced. "While I know that you mean no harm by it, and only do it from the goodness of your hearts, but others in the audience don't like it and it does not tend to improve the character of the entertainment." He was applauded.

Competitors countered Keith with Polite Vaudeville, Refined Vaudeville, Family Vaudeville, Hytone Vaudeville, High-Class Vaudeville, Fashionable Vaudeville, Advanced Vaudeville, Electric Vaudeville, Colossal Vaudeville. In the first two decades of the 20th century there were 1,000 theaters in the United States exclusively devoted to vaudeville, and about 20,000 actors looking for work on the big-time and small-time circuits. The vaudeville circuits "strung America together just as surely as did the railroad tracks," said vaudevillian Joey Adams. The performers referred to each circuit as "time": they were on the Keith Time, Orpheum Time, Pantages Time, doing a turn at two-a-day, three-a-day, and continuous performance houses. One actor, booked for a circuit he hadn't heard of, asked: "What is it? Small-time, medium small-time, big small-time, little big-time, medium big-time, or big-time?" Small-time could be very small—tiny Western circuits the actors nicknamed "The Death Trail" and

"The Aching Heart." Groucho Marx said, "We played towns I would refuse to be buried in today."

The vaudeville actors were importing a kind of time, an urban, continuous, up-tempo time. They had only a few minutes to get their song or joke across. "The effect must be vivid, instantaneous and unmistakable," theater critic Caroline Caffin wrote in 1914. Each gesture counted. It took "the hurried American type" to present in a sketch what was previously spun out over three acts, said comic Joe E. Brown. The vaudevillians were on the frontier of a national culture in the making. The local culture could veto the national product—hiss, stomp, spit tobacco, throw tomatoes, or just "sit on their own hands."

Vaudeville itself, in its form, was continuous—a series of acts shuffled for the best effect, an assembly line of novelties. Every fifteen to thirty minutes brought something new. Magicians, comedians, singers, trapeze acts, tumblers, playlets or sketches, hoofers, contortionists, regurgitators, living statues, animal acts (cockatoos, monkeys, elephants, donkeys, mules, bears, pigs, dogs, cats, and rats), cartoonists, sand artists, shadowgraphers, jugglers of hats, balls, plates, cannonballs . . . dancing jugglers, singing jugglers, comedy jugglers, barrel jumpers, bag punchers, bicyclists, tank acts (swimmers and divers), wirewalkers, sharpshooters, headliners (famous boxers, baseball players, six-day bike-race winners, marathoners, jockeys, billiards champions, champion typists [300 words a minute], Helen Keller and her teacher), mimes, impersonators (doing William Howard Taft and William Jennings Bryan), whistlers, mind readers, male singing quartets, ventriloquists, balancing acts, archers, boomerang throwers, xylophone players, xylophone tap dancers. . . .

In a rare moment, the assembly line and vaudeville were one. In 1916 at Keith's Palace—the premier vaudeville theater, the stage that all vaudeville acts aspired to play—"Twelve Speed Maniacs" assembled a Ford on stage in two minutes.

⁂

With "the Continuous," Benjamin Franklin Keith had found the pulse of the American city. Industrial production was continuous; democracy was a continuous cycle of election-scandal-election. European visitors wrote home that there was always an election going on. "Elections are in the United States as plentiful as revolutions in Peru," the Englishman James Bryce wrote in *The American Commonwealth* (1888). The cities were in a continuous state of building up and tearing down. "*Overturn! Overturn! Overturn!* is the maxim of New York," wrote former mayor Philip Hone in 1845. The greatest undertakings were constantly under construction. When the Erie Canal opened in 1825, the longest canal in the world, its reconstruction began immediately. The British had engineered careful, dead-level, dead-straight runs of track—some of it able to support high-speed trains more than a 150 years later. Yet in America railroads were built as quickly and cheaply as possible and then rebuilt as roadbeds washed out or track was proven unreliable and unsafe. In just fifteen years the Americans built the largest network of railroads in the world. "This country is completely cut up with railroad tracks, telegraphs, canals," Andrew Carnegie wrote home to a cousin in Scotland. "Everything around us is in motion."

In the new industrial world, the blast furnace fired 24 hours a day and some factories worked around the clock. The assembly line was supposed to join thousands of tasks into one continuous motion. Goods moved from the factory to the store in a continuous flow. Interruptions were shortages. Goods did change with the seasons, but it was meant to be seamless: the winter coats arriving after bathing suits as if they were all tied to one thread, like a clown's multicolored handkerchief.

The old life moved to an ancient time: the circle of the seasons, moonrise, sunset, the mystery of darkness, annual spikes in sickness, death, marriage, and conception. The old life had holidays, feast days, mourning, harvest hurry, indolence, and the pooling of slow time. There were crops and chores in season. Entertainment was seasonal. A circus, menagerie, or medicine show might stop by for a few days each summer. But the continuous is a uniform time; it paces forward no matter the season or day. At the end of the 19th century, the continuous still slowed at night and in the summer, and stopped for holidays and Sundays, but those holidays increasingly became uniform goods.

The new order moved to a quicker tempo, promising novelty even as people were employed in repetitive work. In William Dean Howells' novel *Letters Home,* the young hero, recently arrived in New York City, writes home about the scene in the neighborhood of Proctor's 23rd St. Theatre and Keith's Union Square Theatre.

> "I would like to walk you down Twenty-third Street, between Fifth and Sixth avenues, and wake you up to the fact that you have got a country. Only you would think you were dreaming, and it *is* a dream. What impresses me most is the gratis exhibition that goes on all the time, the continuous performance of the streets that you could not get for money any where else, and that here is free to the poorest. In fact, it is *for* the poor. There is one window on Fourteenth Street where the sidewalk is a solid mass of humanity from morning till night, entranced by the fair scene inside; and most of the spectators look as if they had not been to breakfast or dinner, and were not going to supper."

"To everything there is season"—that was the old continuous. In the new continuous, everything was in season everywhere. In the 1870s, a grocer in Lincoln, Nebraska, far from either ocean, could routinely offer his customers oysters. The railroad could bring oysters from the Atlantic, a complete house from Sears & Roebuck in Chicago, or the latest dance and joke from New York City.

II. "On the Clocker"

Keith had begun his circus travels with "wagon shows." "This was vastly superior, from the tourists' standpoint, to traveling by rail and exhibiting only in larger cities and towns," he recalled. "With the wagon show one had all the beauties of the inland country, could see all its types and enjoy the greater hospitality sometimes extended in the remote country districts." The horse was the timekeeper of their days; the horse set the rhythm, limited the distance.

When the power of steam freed travel from animal strength, the shape of time changed. Perceptions changed. "It is a magnificent motion, that one must have felt to appreciate it," Victor Hugo reported in 1837. "Speed is something unheard of. The flowers on the road are no longer flowers, but spots, or rather red or white stripes; no longer points, everything becomes a line; the wheat is a big yellow blur . . . towns, steeples and trees dance and mingle madly on the horizon." Boundaries changed. "I feel as if the mountains and forests of all countries were advancing on Paris," wrote Heinrich Heine, upon the opening of the railroad from Paris to Rouen and Orleans in 1834. "Space is killed by the railways, and we are left with time alone." The *Quarterly Review* imagined the entire English countryside moving closer to the "fireside" of London: "The whole population would, speaking metaphorically, at once advance *en masse*, and place their chairs nearer to the fireside of their metropolis by two-thirds of the time which now separates them from it," the *Review* wrote in 1839. "As distances were thus annihilated, the surface of our country would, as it were, shrivel in size until it became not much bigger than one immense city."

In America, patriotic speakers praised the railroad's "iron bands" for preserving a union of distant states, but in the first years of the railroad the landscape seemed unbound. The old measures—days of travel by horse or oxen, days under sail, or on a narrow canal boat—were thrown out. "Concord shall be taken up and carried ten hours toward the setting sun. The capital of the state shall be virtually transferred from the banks of the Merrimack to banks of the Connecticut," said Dartmouth philosophy professor Charles B. Haddock, addressing a New Hampshire railroad convention in 1843. "The fertile intervals of these beautiful New Hampshire streams shall unite; the intervening mountains shall disappear; the verdant edges of meadows shall knit together; and these glad rivers flow on, side by side, towards the sea."

Railroads "annihilated space and time"; they nullified distance. "All local attachments will be at an end," said one observer in 1830, and the railroads will "set the whole world a-gadding." The coming of the railroad was a "providential event," said Heine, "which swings mankind in a new direction, and changes the color and shape of life."

Morning, noon, and night. This too, changed. At noon on November 18, 1883, Chicagoans moved their clocks back 9 minutes and 33 seconds. The railroads had created time zones. It's as if the railroads had commanded the sun to stand still, said the *Chicago Tribune.*

Before the railroad, each place moved to its own time. Local time was "sun time." When it was 12 noon in Chicago, it was 11:50 a.m. in St. Louis, and 12:18 in Detroit. It was difficult to run a railroad on "sun time." There were hundreds of local times, each city setting its city hall or courthouse clock as it chose. Railroad lines created official time—each line had its own official time, which vexed travelers trying to make connections. Many stations had two clocks, one for railroad time and one for local time. Railroads scheduled trains by more than 70 different time standards in 1872.

The railroads standardized time in 1883, devising four time zones.

(An arrangement the government did not officially recognize until 1918.) International time zones followed in 1884. The Cincinnati *Commercial Gazette* protested. "The Proposition that we should put ourselves out of the way nearly half an hour from the facts so as to harmonize with an imaginary line through Pittsburgh is simply preposterous. . . . Let the people of Cincinnati stick to the truth as it is written by the sun, moon and stars."

The *Louisville Courier-Journal* called the time change a "compulsory lie." A letter to the editor demanded to know "if anyone has the authority and right to change the city time without the consent of the people?" In Maine, the mayor of Augusta refused to run the state capital on "Philadelphia time." The city's voters concurred; three-quarters of the voters defeated the new time in an 1884 referendum. Ohio resisted for nine years, and some Cleveland factories still ran on sun time thirty years after the great reform.

The time of day in Cincinnati or Chicago was no longer a local possession. A trip from New York to Chicago once took more than two weeks, but the arrival of the Michigan Southern on February 20, 1852, shortened the trip to two days. Before the railroad, if a traveler arrived by steamship or stage on the advertised day, it was "on time"; it was common to arrive days late. "Indeed, *time* does not yet seem to enter as an element into Western thought," complained a traveler from the East in 1851. "It answers about as well to do a thing next week as this; to wait a day or two for a boat, as to meet it at the hour appointed; and so on through all the details of life."

The railroad ran "on the tick," "on the clocker." "The locomotive is an accomplished educator. It teaches everybody that virtue of princes we call punctuality," said Benjamin F. Taylor in 1874. "It waits for nobody. It demonstrates what a useful creature a minute is in the economy of things." Taylor commended the "briskness of step and a precision of speech about the people of a railway creation that you never find in a town that is only accessible to a stage-driver."

Standard time, said the New York Herald in 1883, "goes beyond the pursuits of men and enters into their private lives as part of themselves." Benjamin Franklin Keith had his "sort of half dream between waking and sleeping," his epiphany of the Continuous in 1883, the year the railroads changed time.

The new railroad time was part of a push to link clock to clock, to create continuous timekeeping. The railroads had been prodded by a legion of reformers to adopt a uniform time standard. Coordinating time was the great project of the last thirty years of the 19th century, writes Peter Galison in *Einstein's Clocks, Poincare's Maps.* In America, there were "dozens of town councils, railroad supervisors, telegraphers, scientific-technical societies, diplomats, scientists, and observatories all vying to coordinate clocks in different ways." Observatories in Cambridge, Pittsburgh, Cincinnati, Chicago, and St. Louis sold accurate time to subscribers. Each observatory commanded a small empire of time, discouraging local time and preaching against "time anarchy." International conventions set uniform measure and zero longitude. Scientists attempted to coordinate the public clocks of Paris and Vienna in the 1870s by pneumatic tubes. In 1910 radio waves broadcast from the top of the Eiffel Tower began to synchronize clocks around the world. "A world machine" was under construction, writes Galison, "webs of train tracks, telegraph lines, meteorological networks, and longitude surveys all under the watchful, increasingly universal clock system." Some reformers were pushing for one worldwide time zone.

William F. Allen, who had convinced the railroads to adopt standard time, foresaw the day when there could be one master clock. "It would . . . be one of the possibilities of the powers of electricity that the pendulum of a single centrally located clock, beating seconds, could regulate local time-reckoning of every city on the face of the earth."

Here was merging with *there*. Chicago's "now" with Cincinnati's "now." A place could no longer claim just one time. There were many times; there were many nows. They were all valid, said Albert Einstein in 1905. Each observer had his own clock. The more precise and uniform timekeeping became, the more time fragmented. The oldest continuity—the commonsense notion of past, present, and future—was under attack by physics and new inventions. "To those of us who believe in physics," Einstein wrote to the widow of a friend who had recently died, "this separation between past, present, and future is only an illusion, if a stubborn one."

After World War I, silent films began to replace vaudeville. For a while, vaudeville tried to adopt the new amusement, running mixed bills of "vaude film." It was an awkward fit. The films told stories in new ways with montage, parallel editing, double exposures, and slow motion. Time could be reversed and stopped. The film itself, shown at first on hand-cranked projectors, could be slowed or hurried to accompany the theater's organist. Audiences, says historian Stephen Kern, sat in the flickering light, "inspired, horrified, enchanted" by the changing tempo.

Timescape:
The Immortality of Property

I used to search through deeds in an imposing county courthouse, a Beaux Arts "palace for the people." The deed room was big, as long as half a football field, a silent marble chamber lined with thick books that seemed like something from a medieval monastery. All the books were about the same size: legal deeds, contracts, mortgages, debts, attended by clerks with nun-like devotion. The shelves were uniformly spaced, each shelf like an airplane hangar for the books, which sat on metal rollers, numbered binding facing out. Starting with the county's first deed (David Underwood's payment of a gray mare, saddle, and bridle, to cover two years of back pay due to one Christian Charles on July 2, 1794), the books ran through thousands of mortgages, foreclosures, land sales, marriages, separations, divorces, claim settlements, wills, defaulted payments, broken promises, shattered agreements, row after row. It seemed like the same slice of room repeated indefinitely—like those narrow barbershops that echoed toward infinity when you looked into the mirror reflecting the opposite mirror.

The earliest deed books were written in fading brown ink obediently marching across the page in neat penmanship; the later ones were photocopied in reverse, so that the ink is white on black; the more recent ones were gracelessly typed; and the last are on microfiche, a fleck of black plastic. That is, they were the last when I saw them thirty years ago, before computers. At that time there were 2,786 volumes, a vast novel written by anyone who had ever bought or sold, loved or lied, been born or buried, in that one county.

What I remember most is the sound of that room. Clerks—who back then were all women—moved among the rows of books doing title searches. The clerks had an economy of motion: They snapped open a book, its metal binding hitting the table, jotted a few strokes on a legal pad, and then, with one quick wrist motion, slapped it closed, walked back to the shelves, and slid it back onto the rollers. The opening and closing of books was the only sound in the room—a muted metallic *whap* when the book opened and a softer refrain when it was closed.

A deed, says the dictionary, is something that is done; a performed, accomplished, act. But the deed room told another story. These deeds were still talking through the clerks. The opening and closing of the books measured out time. Property may be the biggest clock we have constructed. We have secured an afterlife for money, and we are obsessed with adjusting the laws to ensure this afterlife. Our country is divided into a bundle of "rights"—rights-of-way, property rights, water rights, mineral rights (to dig beneath your lot), air rights (to build above your city lot), pollution rights (or credits to trade poison on the market), and naming rights (a reward for those who have amassed all the rights). Money is immortal. It lives on; we die. It is regular; we are wavering, weak, mortal.

In the 19th century, corporations perfected the afterlife of money. The limited-liability corporation took hold. Before that, corporations were specially chartered, by the Crown in England and the legislature in America, to build roads and canals, establish banks, or for other enterprises in the public interest. Many businesses were partnerships, each partner responsible for his partners' debts. When a partner died, the partnership dissolved. The limited liability corporation protected the stockholders against debt, gave the "corporate body" rights beyond what they had as individuals, and it was immortal. Corporations are another continuous performance.

"Law is often thought of as unfolding in slow patterns," said legal historian Lawrence M. Friedman. "Yet nothing could be more startling than the difference one century made in the law of the business corporation." This change outshone the wonders of 19th-century technology to men like Boston banker Henry Lee Higginson, who said that "incorporation is the most brilliant invention of our past century." Columbia University president Nicholas Murray Butler believed that "the limited liability corporation is the greatest single discovery of modern times," far surpassing "even steam and electricity."

For centuries some inventors were convinced they could discover a source of perpetual motion. They never did; but as an invention, the immortal corporation comes close. Here is the life everlasting on earth, the joint venture that goes on and on.

A Family History of Water

I. Water Is Wealth

I had fourteen miles to go in winter to mill with an ox-team," said one Pennsylvania pioneer in the early 1800s, recalling the struggle to get his corn milled into flour. "The weather was cold and the snow deep; no roads were broken, and no bridges built across the streams. I had to wade the streams and carry the bags on my back. The ice was frozen to my coat as heavy as a bushel of corn. I worked hard all day and got only seven miles the first night, when I chained my team to a tree, and walked three miles to house myself. At the second night I reached the mill." Summer travel wasn't much better: "On the 3rd day of July, I started, with my two yoke of oxen to Jersey Shore to mill, to procure flour," said another Pennsylvania pioneer. "I crossed Pine Creek eighty times going to, and eighty times coming from mill, was gone eighteen days, broke two axle trees to my wagon, upset twice, and one wheel came off in crossing the creek . . . the road was dreadful."

These were common stories: men walking forty miles to the nearest mill carrying hundred-pound bags of grist on their shoulders; communities gathering their grain and sending a party four days by canoe to acquire flour for bread. The first public business of a new town was to build a gristmill and a sawmill.

A small brook, with a fall along its course of only a foot, could power the first waterwheels. A big waterfall was not required; only running water. An undershot wheel, in which the water spun the wheel from underneath, could work on a fall of one foot, and as much as twenty-five feet. Nine-tenths of the water mills in 1835 were built on falls of less than ten feet.

Early mills were all wooden: wooden waterwheels turning heavy wooden gears and shafts; wood thumping wood, creaking along, round and round, up and down, back and forth, at three to five horsepower—a liberating strength. The mills were held together with wooden pins (treenails), wedges, and mortise and tenon joints. Iron was scarce.

Traveling through Massachusetts in 1793, Timothy Dwight counted 262 mills in just one county. By 1840, the first comprehensive federal census to count water mills reported that there were 66,000 mills in America: one for every 245 Americans. This was a significant undercount, neglecting many small mills, said Louis C. Hunter, a historian of industrial power. There were likely 100,000 small mills in the country. "Mechanical power . . . to most Americans was waterpower," wrote Hunter. "The ax produces the log hut," said the commissioner of patents in 1850, "but not till the sawmill is introduced do framed dwellings and villages arise; it is civilization's pioneer machine: the precursor of the carpenter, wheelwright and turner, the painter, joiner, and legions of other professions." Waterpower gave Americans their daily bread and the roof overhead. Water was wealth.

Waterwheels were ancient, little changed over the centuries. What had served the Greeks and the Romans also served Europe in the Middle Ages and Colonial America. Then, from the 1820s to the 1840s, there was a season of innovation: reaction wheels, turbines, and semi-turbines delivered more power; improvements in races, dams, and penstocks captured more water. Mills multiplied. Villages founded on hilltops moved down to the valleys in a quest for waterpower. Millwrights scouted rivers for possible mill seats. Mills began to crowd each other. From the first what Americans wanted from the land was power.

"No one class of inventions, with the exception of stoves, exhibits such a medley of utility and absurdity as the water wheel," said the commissioner of patents in 1843 about the surge of new designs. The interest in waterwheels was long-lived. An engineer in 1891 said, "Every free-born American citizen considers it among his unalienable rights and privileges to invent a patent medicine and a waterwheel, and he usually does both with usual ignorance of and indifference to the laws of both hygiene and hydraulics!"

Water was hoarded. Nearly every pond, lake, river, and brook was altered. Dams were built, swamps and pastures were flooded. The "unspoiled" lakes, beloved by summer visitors today, and the "pristine" ponds in nature sanctuaries, have a hidden industrial past. They were reservoirs. Impounded water was the coal heap of the early 1800s. The landscape was reshaped in a quest for power. The more water a mill claimed, the more machines it could run. Water was progress.

Small factory villages were built by waterfalls, redeeming land thought to be worthless, as one promotional pamphlet said in 1849:

> "In the most rocky and desolate situations, avoided by all human beings since the settling of the Pilgrims as the image of loneliness and bareness, amid rocks and stumps and blasted trees, there is a waterfall. Taking its stand here, the genius of our age calls into almost instantaneous life a bustling village. Here factories erected in this barren waste, and suddenly a large population is gathered. For this population everything necessary to the social state is to be created. The past contributes nothing."

Waterpower, this inheritance from the ancients, was finite, but it was plentiful. For 250 years falling water was America's chief source of mechanical energy. In New England, hundreds of small factory villages arose, empires built on falling water.

II. Choreographer of the Waters

In hurricane season Chick Colony pays attention to the weather in the Caribbean. Chick lives in Harrisville, New Hampshire. He's not interested in the local forecast; he's waiting for the end of the forecast, when the weatherman sweeps his arm hundreds of miles south down the Atlantic seaboard, where he points to a hurricane wheeling toward some small Caribbean island. When a hurricane starts tracking north, Chick heads out to the dam.

Chick's given name is John J. Colony, III. No one calls him that, mostly because his father was John J. Colony Jr. and the name is too formal. Four generations of his family ran the Cheshire Mills in Harrisville before it went out of business in 1970. When his father was in his eighties, Chick became the choreographer of the watershed. He also looks after the mill village of Harrisville, a handsome redbrick ensemble resembling a small liberal arts college. "The factory under the elms," as one historian called it, seems like an idealized picture of itself (even though it had, until recently, just one surviving elm).

Whenever I visit I have a feeling of arriving after an evacuation. The tall mill buildings, shaped by technology, have the upright bearing of a thrifty, church-going, laconic New England. The buildings are austere, serious; the bell towers have authority.

It is reassuring to find these poised and graceful buildings calmly reflected in the water. It is like meeting a man of his word. But these mills, now turned to quieter purposes, are deceiving. Though we don't recognize it, Harrisville is a creation of moneymaking. We recognize such sites when we see the mills of Lowell, Ford's River Rouge factory, or the cooling towers of a nuclear plant, but here we are fooled—just as we are fooled by Lake Nubanusit.

The outlet dam on Lake Nubanusit is a small thing. The floodgates are only three feet across. The top of the dam is 11.8 feet.

Flashboards, old rough lumber, add another six inches. The gatehouse is a wooden shed, home to a few bats and some wasps.

Inside Chick looks down at the top of the dam, the new aluminum gates and the old flashboards. There is a wheel on top to open the gates. He looks at a water-level gauge and the water running over the top. He pokes a long rod in and pulls it out. It's wet a handspan or more, about six inches. There is plenty of water flowing out. He has already removed a couple of flashboards, so he decides to leave it for a while. He is like a baker testing a cake.

The errand and the warning seem mismatched. A storm hundreds of miles across, a thousand miles away, sends Chick a mile out of town over dirt roads to a hut the size of a toolshed where he might turn an old iron wheel as some bats look on. This is not the heroic dam—Hoover stopping the Colorado—that stars in encyclopedias and documentaries. This is just one of thousands of small New England dams, a legacy of the age of waterpower.

The act of adjusting the dam also seems a bit mismatched. He moves a board or two, or turns the wheel a little and adjusts the water level for a watershed that includes hundreds of houses along the shores of several large ponds and lakes. It's as if by adjusting the television reception you were adjusting the world and not a picture of the world.

Behind this small gatehouse lies a 715-acre lake, and flowing into it, attended by another dam, is a smaller 180-acre pond. These flow a mile and a half through a great meadow toward a third pond and the third Colony dam.

Chick and his family own this water. Or rather they own the legal part of the water—the part of the water that is power, the part that isn't "wetness" or the loons, or the sunsets in the memories of generations of summer people. They own the measure of the water, the right to control it. This legal right trumps all other rights on the lake, and this makes some people angry. Everyone has an opinion about the water level on Nubanusit. There are file folders at the Dam Bureau up in Concord bulging with letters of complaint going back to 1938, petitions, and the records of hearings. The homeowners' association on the lake wants the water level high so their docks float. But those living at the end of the lake, in the town of Nelson, want it at a different level than those at the other end of the lake, three and a half miles away in Hancock. The Audubon Society wants the water level held steady for the loons. One year the loons laid their eggs late and the society asked Chick to delay lowering the lake.

The Colonys are keenly aware of the many claims on this water, and what serious weather can do to all this fine-tuning. Chick, like his father, does not see just a lake or a brook—he sees a watershed. He sees water on the move from Spoonwood Pond and Lake Nubanusit to Harrisville Pond to Skatutakee Lake and on to the Goose Brook, which meets the Contoocook in Peterborough and then flows north to the Merrimack and finally the Atlantic. Few people know where the rain that runs off their roof is headed. (About four miles from the Harrisville mills, in Nelson, two of the six major watersheds in New Hampshire touch. Parke Hardy Struthers at Merriconn Farm liked to say that a drop of rain falling on one side of his roof was destined for the Connecticut River and on the other side, the Merrimack. He combined the names for his farm.)

Chick has an eye for waterpower. He once told me that Keene—the "big city" nearby, with a population of 22,500—would have been an ideal site for a large reservoir. An industrialist could have flooded twenty square miles of the valley and powered quite a large operation. I doubt that anyone else has ever cast an antediluvian eye on Keene and seen the broad Main Street, the Civil War statue in Central Square, and the white spire of the First Church under water.

But our era values waterfront, not waterpower. When confronted with the idea that someone owns the water of their beloved summer place, ordinary red-meat, free-hand-of-the-marketplace Republicans are befuddled. Who can own the water? Some hidden tree-hugger rises up in them. They think this fine, long pond was the work of God, not the Harrises and Colonys whose dams created the lake they know. They believe it to be Eden. But Lake Nubanusit is an industrial reservoir. Each day they swim or canoe in an early 19th-century version of the coal heap and the cooling tower. Water was power, not recreation.

In this small watershed are the echoes of the 19th-century fights over water rights. Everyone has a claim. Chick has inherited a water-power kingdom in the age of the leisure economy. Owning water—three dams in this case—is all liability. That's what sends Chick out to the dam on a sunny fall day—the liability of history: the memories of the great New England Hurricane of 1938.

III. '38 and After

"We get into September, we see any rain at all, we open our gates just as fast as we can," Chick's father, John, told me a few years before he died. There are three large ponds and three smaller ponds "above us," he says, listing, in addition to Spoonwood and Nubanusit, Shadrach, Tenney, Tolman, and Harrisville ponds. "They all come together in Harrisville. If you fly over this area, you'd be astounded by how many lakes and ponds are involved. It's a good watershed. It gets a lot of good storage—there's a lot of snowfall. You see, we're at an altitude of 1,700 feet and snowfall lasts; builds up all winter. It is quite unusual to see that many lakes in a smaller area."

On its short nine-mile journey from Lake Nubanusit through Harrisville to Peterborough, the Goose Brook falls 600 feet. (On most maps today it's the Nubanusit Brook, but the Colonys stick to the old name.) In 1870 the brook powered eight mills employing more than 900 workers. From the air, the brook is hard to distinguish. You wouldn't select it as a route for a lazy canoe trip, let alone associate it with the word *power.* It meanders like a newsboy's paper route. Yet in the time before there were towns and water rights, the brook fell through a steep ravine, wild enough to discourage the first white settlers. In the lottery to distribute the land for the town-in-the-making known as Monadnock Number Three, John Usher had the misfortune to draw Range 10, lots 13 and 14—the ravine's location. There was no place to farm; there was scarcely a level place for a plow. He gave up the wasteland that would become Harrisville.

The Colonys had the waterpower appraised by an expert in 1903. John Humphrey, a turbine builder, considered these highland lakes and ponds to be "perhaps the best and most reliable waterpower of its size to be found in New England or elsewhere." A typical watershed has a land-to-water ratio of twenty to one, but with so many ponds in such a small area, the ratio here is four to one. John Colony called it a "flashy" watershed—a sudden storm could catch the Colonys with the reservoirs too full, and the damage downstream could be tremendous. An increase of one foot in the level of Lake Nubanusit will, when released, raise Harrisville Pond three feet. Humphrey issued a warning:

"Permit me to call your attention to the great risk incident to entering upon a season of heavy rainfall with the Nubanusit Lake nearly or quite filled—as by so doing the stream is not only returned to its primitive uncontrollable turbulence, but has an additional element of danger in the probability of a breakage of the dam, which would let loose a body of water likely to do much damage at Harrisville and other places on the stream . . . for this reason it is much safer and better to have the pond three feet below high-water mark in September."

Water has a family history in Harrisville. "Abel Twitchell lived in that white house right over there, the first house in town, just restored.

Started a sawmill village and used the waterfall here," said John, sitting in his house on Harrisville Pond. "He and his brother owned all the lots around this lake. So there was no formality of having to buy the water rights from all the others. They owned it all just by owning the whole lake. That was about 1790 that water was first used."

From the back porch of John's house, the view straight up the pond shows no other houses. The porch looks north to where the Goose Brook enters the pond after its trip from the outlet dam on Lake Nubanusit. It's like some deep woods view—another deception of a state that had once managed to be both industrial and rural. Close by, out a side window, is Chick's brick house. "Bethuel Harris, by the way, when he came here from Providence, he married Twitchell's daughter and built that house right there," John said, pointing to Chick's house. "His sons built these other brick houses around. This was Cyrus Harris' house, and he was the oldest brother. Milan Harris is across the street." He finished the tour by noting the houses of the other sons. This was John Colony's neighborhood.

The names as John says them are like the clutch, pinion, and gears of a clock, each meeting the next, advancing the time. Twitchell to Harris to Harris to Colony. The names on the deeds and the mills keep the time.

English Common Law—the law that came ashore with the first settlers—said that no one could own what runs free—"Running water is not in its nature private property," as one English judge said. Rivers were shared in common under the first laws of the colonies. Millers were required to protect a farmer's meadows from flooding. A landowner whose land was flooded could remove the nuisance himself, breaking the dam with pry bars or gunpowder, instead of calling on lawyers and judges to win redress. A series of Mill Acts, first in the 18th and early 19th centuries in Massachusetts and Rhode Island, then later in New Hampshire, changed that. The mills had the right-of-way; they had eminent domain. The mill owners could flood and destroy fishing spots and hayfields, could alter the course of a non-navigable stream, as long as they paid limited damages. A 1796 Massachusetts mill act capped the damages at four pounds per year. The millers could flood first, and pay later. They could avoid paying any damages by proving that the landowner benefited from flooding. Dam breaking was outlawed.

Mills were given "virtually unlimited discretion" to destroy property worth far more than any benefit that might accrue, said legal historian Morton J. Horwitz. "From the time they were extended to cotton mills, the mill acts represented the most extreme invasion of the eminent domain power into private activities, as well as the most blatant instance of the ruthless exercise of that power to bring about redistributions of wealth," said Horwitz.

Water was a commodity; its ownership was contested. Water rights were hotly litigated: fishermen vs. millers, lumberman vs. millers, farmers vs. millers, millers vs. millers. When the rights of two mills conflicted, the larger mill usually won. The owner of an upstream mill sued a large mill in Lawrence, Massachusetts, because the Lawrence dam had backed up water, flooding his waterwheels and destroying his mill privilege. The Lawrence mill defended itself by saying its act of incorporation gave it the right to take—or destroy—private property by eminent domain. The company was acting in the public interest. Chief Justice Lemuel Shaw of the Massachusetts Supreme Judicial Court agreed, saying that this "great mill power" was an "object of great public interest." Time was standardized in the 19th century and so were rivers. Once time was a river. Now time was money.

The Lawrence dam—then the world's largest—would have been illegal under common law just fifty years earlier. The economy was changing, and so was the law. Water was private property; it no longer flowed free.

On green, eye-ease ledger paper, John had drawn up a corporate flow chart, little rectangular boxes linked with lines, to show a true accounting of who owned the water rights, from top to bottom, a cascade of names falling like water.

"These are all the deed references," he said, starting with Breed Batchelder in 1762. "And so it came down through Bethuel Harris to Milan Harris, who had that mill right there, and Cyrus Harris, who lived here and built the stone mill." The chart continues to the Colonys' Cheshire Mills, and after that, John Colony. "These things go right down through the generations like any other piece of property," he said. (And "just like any woodlot or house," dams are taxed.)

"My family was in the textile business in Keene: Faulkner & Colony. That started around 1815. Equal partnership between two families." About thirty-five years later, the Colonys were looking for a new mill. "Cyrus Harris decided to separate from the other Harrises; started another mill. He built the stone mill down here, the Granite mill. And unfortunately, or fortunately for us, I guess, just about the time this brand new empty mill was finished, he died. What they called consumption in those days. Tuberculosis. So my family, independently of their partners in Keene, came over here and bought this brand-new, empty stone mill. Bought new machinery and machined it up.

"When my family came and bought this mill here, everybody needed more power. And so my family, with the covenants of the others, but independently financed, went up and put a dam in Spoonwood. And that added to the storage for the dry month of August. They went around and paid all the farmers around the lake for the privilege of raising the water up to a certain fixed point." The land was mostly meadows and cow pastures.

"Nubanusit was just a series of three smaller lakes. They gradually raised the dams; they needed more power. Of course the more they raised them, the higher the level went and the more the storage was. That was quite an incentive—it was a prospering industry—to develop that capacity and height.

"It was a help to all these other mills. The Harrises still ran that mill and there was another Harris, who had some partners, ran the mill down the hill. At one time there were four or five users right in a row here in Harrisville. Somebody dumped the water from his turbine, it went down to the next guy, and the next guy." In dry times the mills squabbled with each other, sometimes in court. In flood times, the mills were sued by farmers for lost pasture and by the town for submerged roads.

Harrisville ran on water, but the town was created by the railroad. The village that grew up around the mills straddled the town line between Dublin and Nelson. (The line ran right through Chick's house.) When the farmers in those towns refused to subscribe to the new railroad coming through, Milan Harris, with the swift aid of the state legislature, created Harrisville in 1870, taking parts of the other two towns with him. Harrisville was "railroaded" into existence.

In John's telling, all of Harrisville's history was contemporary. "My family came over here, to Harrisville, in 1852," he said. "There was one farmer that didn't sell us the water rights in the 1860s. Breed Batchelder, the first owner of the water rights, was a Tory; he didn't last long around here," he said, making it sound as if a moving van—Tory Van Lines—had come for Batchelder recently. Of some other mill owners who were early partners of the Harrises, he said, "They were strangers around here." In a phrase, John Colony could take you from 1763 and Breed Batchelder to 1970, when his family's mill closed.

He took the long view. Once he was going through a stack of legal deeds with his lawyer. The deeds had been found in an old strong box.

"When was this deed passed?" the lawyer asked.

"Fifty-three," said John.

"Fifty-three?" asked the lawyer. "Fifty-three—I was your lawyer in '53. I don't remember that."

"Eighteen fifty-three," said John.

When Chick asked him what he thought about Pat Buchanan's run in the 1996 New Hampshire presidential primary, he said, "One President Buchanan is enough." (Back in 1856 the Democratic Colonys had welcomed President James Buchanan's victory. Celebrating millworkers had fired a cannon at rival Republican Milan Harris' mill, breaking some windows. When Milan protested, the "Buchanan boys" punched him, or so went Milan's case in court.)

At the start of the 20th century, John's father, John Sr., took the early morning train from Keene, arriving in Harrisville at 5:45 a.m. On dark winter mornings he napped on a cot in his office until the waterpower was turned on at 7 a.m. A thrifty Yankee didn't start the wheels turning just for his own use.

Thrift was a steady habit. As late as 1945, the company did not employ stenographers or bookkeepers. The Colonys did their own paperwork by hand. The Keene and Harrisville offices had no typewriters. And there was no telephone in the Harrisville office before 1928. The mills and the workers' boardinghouse were known for their cleanliness.

John began working in the mill in 1937, after Harvard and a European tour with his friends. He had wanted to go to Harvard's business school for a year, but his father was getting on in years at age 73, and he thought it prudent to stay home and learn the mill business. He spent two months working in the different departments of the woolen mill, including the carding room, the dye room, and the spinning room. "I got to be a pretty good mule spinner," he said. He had a strong affection for the machinery and the cloth. "They were beautiful fabrics. And they were tough, really tough," he says, recalling the cloth they made for major league baseball team uniforms.

After his apprenticeship he was put in charge of a payroll of up to 450 employees, which was paid out weekly in cash brought in on the train from Keene.

As a mill owner, John continued the Colonys' practical tradition. He was a "hands-on manager" long before the business schools burdened us with the term, fixing broken machinery and repairing the mills. His sons were required to work summer maintenance jobs at the mills. One summer his son George was painting a building when he saw his father, then sixty years old, way up on the cupola of a mill. John had tied a ladder to one of the posts and climbed up with a paint can tied to his belt. He believed that it was too dangerous for anyone else.

In John's second year at work, the hurricane of September 21, 1938, hit; the Goose Brook flooded Harrisville, just as Humphrey had warned thirty-five years earlier. All that water "above" the town was coming their way. It had rained for two weeks before the hurricane. "There were tremendous floods everywhere. We'd been watching Harrisville—the lakes were full, the floodgates were open, and the water was still coming up," said John. Nelson's road agent saw the wind driving twelve-foot waves over the Nubanusit dam. On one side of the lake, eighty percent of the trees were blown down. "We were doing all we could do to get the water through. Of course it had to pass under the mill. We used sandbags to bolster up the banks. Water was going around both ends of the Harris mill. It was wiping out the roads down below, and going in the windows of the Granite mill. It was pretty bad."

It was far worse downstream in Peterborough. "Right in the middle of that hurricane they called us up and wanted to know if we could stop the flow of water from Harrisville. Peterborough begged us to close the floodgates because they were having so much trouble." There was nothing John could do.

∞

"What you have to remember first is that nobody expected anything to happen," said Everett S. Allen, who saw the hurricane in New Bedford, Massachusetts. Disasters happened in faraway places where they "built their houses out of straw." The hurricane arrived without preamble, without forecast or hype.

There's never been a hurricane in these latitudes, people said: It's a line storm, a three days' blow at the equinox. In Rhode Island they had lunch and watched the surf crash and sent their children back to school. It can't happen here, people said.

Hour by hour, the hurricane remade New England, each town a variation of wind and flood, and occasionally fire. "Keene [New Hampshire] is a shambles. Its elms were its pride. Today they are its sorrow," Ralph G. Page wrote in his diary. Thousands of big trees were down in the city. "Wheelock Park looks like the Argonne forest. Its beautiful pines are piled like huge jackstraws... Cut off from the rest of the world except by short wave radio, Keene is a world by itself tonight."

In Peterborough, the Goose Brook raced into the Contoocook. "I was shocked at the size of the little Contoocook—no longer the gentle, reedy stream where I had fished as a kid, but a veritable Missouri—turgid, yellow, hissing and muttering downstream," said Edwards Park. He had walked into town with his father on errands. His father, too, had thought this was a line storm.

The Contoocook jumped its banks, flooding Main Street, and the town started to burn. The fire began in a granary. "Great clouds of flying debris, all in flame" pushed by the wind burned down three blocks. Firefighters ran with a slack hose through the flooded street. "Gripping the hose, the gang charged the surging flood. It swept them cleanly off their feet, one by one, and hurled them downstream, and we watched aghast," said Park. They tried and were knocked down again before they got the hose through. The firefighters stood in floodwaters up to their hips all night. The fire threatened the entire town.

∞

The day after was sky-blue, perfect—like heaven, people said. "I remember on that day how spent one emerged, how quiet people were, as nature was finally quiet, and how incredible it was, not only that the storm was over, but that it could have occurred at all," said Everett S. Allen.

The world had changed overnight, and it would change again. People understood now that hurricanes could invade New England. "We thought we were safe in our cold north from their furies. It will take us a long time to recover our faith in the security of the northland," said Cornelius Weygandt. The 1938 hurricane was one of the worst disasters in American history, surpassing the San Francisco earthquake in death, injury, and destruction.

Three days after the hurricane, *The Keene Evening Sentinel* published an emergency edition, printed on a press rigged to a gas engine. In four pages devoted to news about their wrecked and isolated city, the back page had a bulletin from the Associated Press: "War Appears Inevitable." Prime Minister Neville Chamberlain's appeasement talks with Hitler were failing. "France, Russia, Germany and Czechoslovakia are reported ready to enter the conflict immediately." A week later, Hitler was allowed to seize part of Czechoslovakia; the world would be at war within a year.

IV. Leisure Power

After the flood, after the war: peacetime, summertime. More than sixty years gone by, a new century. Two young men in their late twenties were portaging their canoe over the small dam at Spoonwood Pond. Their talk turned to the man who owned the dam. "All he talks about is the Hurricane of '38," one of them said. "Thirty-eight—Thirty-eight."

His friend answered him, "You should've been out in the woods with John," a trapper and tracker. "He was always talking about it: In '38 this was all blown down; in '38 nothing was standing. You should've seen this in '38." The pond sparkled in the summer morning. They looked around as if to say: What's the big deal?

Waterpower, having changed our entire landscape, is nearly invisible to modern observers. Waterpower created Lake Nubanusit, but leisure power now stakes its claim and the mill legacy is all but forgotten.

After World War I, the Cheshire Mills began to retire its waterpower. Electricity arrived in 1924, yet water supplied two-thirds of the mills' power until 1947. The mills closed in 1970, a bleak year for the textile industry; 54 other New England mills closed that year. (There were 95,000 broadlooms in the United States at one point. "We figured if it ever got to 20,000, the industry would be stabilized. So we patiently waited," said John. "It got down to 5,000 looms—it wasn't damn hot then.") In March 1971, *Yankee* magazine's usual "House for Sale" article featured Harrisville as a "Town for Sale." The Colonys and their friends began Historic Harrisville, preserving the village not as a museum theme park, but by finding compatible businesses for the empty mills.

The Cheshire Mills had closed, but the Colonys still owned the water. (By deed, the Colonys own the right to draw 11 feet, 10 inches. The deed defines a full pond as 13 feet, 1 inch.) This deed was contested in a battle between leisure power and waterpower. It was a kind of civil Hatfield and McCoy feud, with a New England cold defiance substituted for gunfire. Petitioning the state for a hearing on the lake's level in 1977, The Nubanusit Lake Association said, "Our specific complaint is as follows: The level of the water of the lake varies considerably and in an erratic fashion during the months of June through October, when the lake is used for recreational purposes and as a water supply for cottages on its shores." Or as one petitioner wrote, "We have been on the lake since 1950 and the water level has been most annoying these 26 years." Add to this letters complaining of John Colony's "seemingly irrational control" of the lake and suggestions that he was a fading Yankee king holding onto the dam as his "last vestige of power."

John Colony's answer was patient, direct, and a little biting: "The basic problem is that Spoonwood and Nubanusit are very large lakes in an extremely small watershed and, as such, approach very nearly the function of true reservoirs and not the unchanging lakes of great beauty that all newcomers feel that they have discovered." This was his answer in each decade.

Before the last public hearings about the lake's level in 1993, the lake association surveyed its members, asking them to check one of the following:

__ I prefer the seasonal level range from 11'9" to 12'6"

__ Other (Please specify)___________

__ I prefer winter level to be 11' or above

__ Other (Please specify)___________

__ I would like to see the seasonal level continue until October 15 rather than September 15 [Favored by the majority.]

The lake association and the Colonys were not living in the same place. They had two different concepts of the landscape. The map the cottage dwellers along Nubanusit would draw and the one John or Chick would draw were different. For half a century the debate had been the same. I say lake and you say reservoir. I say natural and you say man-made. I say float my boat until Labor Day and you say 1938.

The country began with waterpower, with work that was local and seasonal. Waterpower was tied to a place. It was that place translated by dams, wheels, belts, and labor to make flour, lumber, cloth. A few feet farther from the falls, away from the river—a few feet and you don't have power. Waterpower was not portable. This may be its most antique aspect. In the 19th century, mills sat alongside, and across, brooks and rivers. The size of the mill was limited by the amount of water available—each shaft, pulley, and belt that ran from the main wheel to the machinery wasted power. This "millwork," as it is known, could consume twenty to fifty percent of the power just to travel several hundred feet. Today power is transmitted; the turbines spinning from Niagara turn on a light thousands of miles away. In the age of waterpower, mill cities had to be built close to the source.

Power was local and limited. It was limited to the river, which could run dry—the entire machine, all those linked machines, shut down. A severe drought in 1879 and 1880 had stopped mills from Maine to Virginia. There were more than 400 mill towns in New England facing hard times. In Harrisville, the water failed in the fall of 1879 and again in the fall of 1880. The mills shut down for three months each time, and most of the workers left. Those who stayed wouldn't have much to see them through the winter.

This drought, and earlier droughts in 1866 and 1870, exposed the weakness of waterpower: It wasn't reliable. Even in years of normal rainfall, with dams and reservoirs, mills had less water in summer and fall. Waterpower could be improved with efficiencies, by installing new turbines, fixing gates and sluices, belting and machinery, but it remained at the mercy of the weather. Waterpower moved to village time, to agricultural time. Small rivers and brooks slowed to a trickle, and when they did, there were other jobs to be done. But the tempo of American life had changed after the Civil War. Modern times demanded steady production and large operations. If your laborers were idle too long, you would lose them. Smaller mills were abandoned and larger mills turned increasingly to steam power.

Capitalism is, of course, portable. It's about finding the cheapest way to produce things—it reduces the cost of production and transportation. It finds a way to shrink distances, "annihilate space and time," as they said repeatedly in the 19th century, to get materials and markets together. If your factory isn't the cheapest way, the show moves on. Waterpower doesn't move. It's half old-time craft and half modern production. It was standardized, but could run only when there was water. This is a halfway step from craft to standard production by standard time.

To the Colonys, water is power, it's money at work: water = mill time = cloth. To the summer people, water is leisure, it's money earned. Water is the reward. It's time to relax, to play. Look at what I bought (or inherited)—this lake!

There are two different timekeepers in this place. Waterpower wrenched time and place once and leisure power wrenches it again. Time is shaping the maps here. The industrial time that shaped the land is invisible to the summer people. "What time is this place?" as city planner Kevin Lynch once asked. It depends on which clock you have in mind.

Timescape:

"I Opened the Store as Usual"

On January 1, 1898, Clinton Preston Davis, a high school sophomore, began to keep a diary. He was industrious, if not the top student or speller. Davis was president of the Class of 1900 at his high school in Antrim, New Hampshire, and sometimes made the honor roll. (There were twelve in his class, the largest yet in the school's short history.)

He went on to the Mount Hermon School in Northfield, Massachusetts, but came home to work in the family business after only a semester. His mother, Clara, a widow, ran a store selling "gents furnishings, hats, caps and children's clothing." In his first years out of school, almost every diary entry begins: "I opened the store as usual." Each day Clinton noted the temperature when he rose in the morning and at midday, recording it as was the custom: 34/0—34 degrees above zero. With only six lines assigned to each date in his pocket diary, Clinton was limited to four or five sentences:

Feb. 21, 1902 Fri. 5/0 - 28/0 Cloudy, Warm

I opened the store as usual. I studied some. I carried a weather report up to Miss Perkins at School. I went down to the shop and saw Granvill Whitney about last year's ball team. In the evening Everett gave me a ticket to the School entertainment in the Town Hall for Washington's Birthday.

Turn the pages forward or back and it's much the same:

April 4, 1901 Thurs. 34/0 - 40/0 Cloudy, Warm

I opened the store as usual. When mamma came down we arranged a showcase with suspenders . . .

April 10, 1901 Wed. 36/0 - 46/0 Clear, Warm

I opened the store as usual. Then I brushed all the boy's suits. . .

He goes "up street" with a delivery. He goes "down street" with a delivery. Trade is light—"There were not very many around to trade all day"—and once in a while it is busy, as would be expected on the day before Christmas. He writes "duns" to collect on their bills. Clothing drummers (traveling salesmen) call on them. He studies "shorthand, arithmetic typewriting and telegraphy."

The diary moves along like a clock with only one hand: *opened-the-store, opened-the-store,* but day by day Clinton's busy life emerges for the reader. Once he opened the store, his mother would come down around noon, leaving him free. Country villages lived a life apart. Each village was a small world, left mostly alone for its social life. Clinton went out many evenings to lectures, to dances such as the Fireman's Ball, to singing school, to play whist at the whist club, to wait on tables at church suppers, and to the Y.P.S.C.E. (Young Peoples Society for Christian Endeavor). On Sundays he pumped the organ and went to Sunday School.

Jan. 22, 1902 Wed. 40/0 - 50/0 Rain, Warm

I opened the store as usual . . . In the evening Fannie and I went to the last in the lecture course "The Hawthorne Musical Club." It was a fine entertainment.

He went to the other lectures that winter, including the Apollo Quartet and the Thespian Dramatic Company, described by the local newspaper as "a company of highly educated artists presenting a series of plays from the works of our best authors in a condensed form."

Sometimes he was on stage taking part in a debate:

Jan. 24, 1902 Fri. 25/0 - 34/0 Clear, Cool

I opened the store as usual . . . In the evening was the Lyceum. Harriman and I won on the negative from Ray Burnham and Fred Parmenter. Question was that the Chinese should be permanently excluded from the U.S.

And he was enlisted in the temperance cause:

July 27, 1902 Sun. 60/0 - 70/0 Clear, Warm

I went to church and Sunday school as usual. . . . In the evening there was a temperance concert in our church by all the churches. I had to speak.

That fall Antrim emptied out to go hear the great temperance crusader Carrie Nation speak at a fair in a nearby town. Clinton went but makes no mention of her. ("Dressed entirely in white, with a white shawl over her shoulders, her face bearing an uncanny resemblance to the souvenir hatchets she sold, she lambasted . . . all political parties except the Prohibition Party . . . and characterized the Republicans of New Hampshire as a gang of anarchists," says the Antrim town history.) Clinton's diaries are true to their form; they are an accounting. Any description, speculation, emotion, even gossip, would be out of place, just as it would on a ledger sheet. He kept his monthly expenses with his diary—a Valentine card shows up as an expense in 1906 but doesn't get a mention in the diary. (The sole exception is when he despaired of Mount Hermon in his first weeks, writing: "I am sick of this place.")

During the day, in winter, he would go for sleigh rides and ice skate, as he did on Christmas day, after "the biggest day we ever had in the store."

Dec. 25, 1902 Thurs. 14/0 - 20/0 Cloudy, Cool

I opened the store in the A.M. as usual. Then I went out skating. It snowed some in the P.M. but we boys were all out skating . . .

Feb. 12, 1902 Wed. 9/0 - 20/0 Clear, Warm

I opened the store as usual. I took my usual studies. In the afternoon I went to a sleigh ride over to Deering and back through Hillsboro Village. It is fine sleighing . . .

In the summer he did some chores in the yard and garden, rode his "wheel" (bicycle), played tennis and baseball.

Aug. 9, 1902 Sat. 60/0 - 80/0 Clear, Warm

I opened the store as usual. . . . In the afternoon I pitched against the Peterboros and they won 11 to 8, it was a very good game. There were not many around to trade.

He also made excursions to climb Mount Monadnock, about twenty miles away. The return trip in the summer of 1902, he noted, took four hours by horse and wagon. He went with the "teachers," a group of women, some of whom he knew from his class. Two women, Fannie and Susie, from his high school class, often accompanied him to lectures, parties, and picnics. Susie sometimes called on him.

Feb. 1, 1902 Sat. 17/0 - 30/0 Cloudy, Warm

I opened and swept out the store. It commenced to snow about five. . . . Mama went home at 5:30 I closed the store. Then went over to Fannies to a party of teachers. We had peanut hunt candy pull etc. I got home at 12.

He didn't marry either Fannie or Susie. Fannie, an honor-roll student and a teacher, never married. Your prospects were limited when there were only two boys in your graduating class of twelve, and only thirteen hundred people in your town.

Clinton had his eye on the new things coming along. He was a photographer, and developed and mounted his photos, some of which he sold. In his son's words, "Clinton lived and thrived, on the cutting edge of technology." He knew Morse code and sometimes filled in at the railroad depot at Elmwood Junction.

Aug. 18, 1902 Mon. 40/0 - 60/0 Cloudy, Warm

I opened the store as usual. . . . In the afternoon Everett and I rode over to Elmwood to hear the telegraphs go. I rode on Arthur Nesmith's wheel. We got some apples at Tenneys.

Nov. 4, 1902 Tues. 31/0 - 60/0 Clear, Warm

I opened the store as usual. I was at the election about all day. This town went democratic. Will Ingram brought the main line of telegraph up street and we took off returns all night. I went to sleep in the store. Stayed there till morning.

Clinton built a network of telegraph lines around town and then started a local telephone company with his friend, the town barber Norman Morse, and wired the village. A long-distance company had already run a line to the village. "All I am thinking about now is telephone lines for Antrim," Clinton wrote.

Judging by the entries for 1902, the phone equipment needed constant attention. Clinton and Norman were busy moving wires, building switchboards, fixing telephones, installing a telegraph and telephone at the depot, collecting phone bills, and talking about phones with the long distance linemen and the New England Telephone Company, which tried to buy their small operation. (It was quite small: "The selectmen tried to tax our telephone line but found we did not own enough to tax," Clinton noted.)

Aug. 8, 1902 Fri. 56/0 - 70/0 Cloudy, Warm

I opened the store as usual. . . . We had a heavy thunder shower at noon and it burnt out some telephone fuses. I tried to find the ground in our line but could not. In the evening there was a hearing for some hitching posts out front.

Aug. 22, 1902 Fri. 54/0 - 66/0 Cloudy, Cool

I opened the store as usual. I wound the bell coil that broke on my bell. In the afternoon Morse and I fixed the machine that Abbott brought down. . . . I shall wind the induction coil of Abbott's over . . .

Oct. 2, 1902 Thurs. 55/0-70/0 Clear, Warm

I opened the store as usual. I changed all my wires down stairs by twisting them together and bringing them up in a new place . . .

Oct. 22, 1902 Wed. 20/0 - 40/0

I opened the store as usual. There was a long distance man here all day talking with us. The electric wire and telephone wires at Bennington got connected and did quite a little damage to the long distance phone.

Nov. 13, 1902 Thurs. 40/0 - 50/0 Cloudy, Cool

I opened the store as usual. It rained a cold sleety rain all day. Morse and I worked on our new switchboard. In the evening I put it up. Archie Nay got a lamp and sodering iron down to the shop and sodered for us. It did not work after we got it done.

Nov. 17, 1902 Mon. 36/0 - ?/0 Cloudy, Warm

. . . Morse and I fixed the switchboard so it works fine, we also varnished it . . .

This goes on for years. It's impossible to tell how many subscribers they had, but phone service seems to have been no more than a sometimes thing. It was a full-time job to keep Clinton's village empire of telegraph and telephone humming. Each link was the weakest link:

July. 5, 1901 60/0 - 80/0 Clear, Warm

I opened the store as usual. Our depot telegraph line would not work so Ingram and Morse tried to find it but couldn't. . . . After dinner we started down in swimming and on the way watched for trouble on the line. We found it. Someone had cut the wire and tied in a piece of rope. We mended it. . . . It rained some as we went home. I got only one egg today and one yesterday. We did not go in swimming.

The big news of 1902 in Antrim was the burglary of the post office. Clinton recorded it:

Sept. 2, 1902 67/0 - 80/0 Clear, Hot

I opened the store as usual. I stayed there all morning. The P.O. was broken into and the safe blown open and all the money taken. The robbers also took Colby's horse and wagon. They were followed to Peterboro but they took train there and went to Winchendon. I threw in a load of Abbott's wood.

That was about all there was to tell, though people talked about it for years. *The Antrim Reporter* adds a few details about the heist. The robbers first stole a sledgehammer and several drills from the blacksmith and a horse blanket from the Antrim House stables. They threw the horse blanket—wet—over the safe to deaden the sound and blew open the door. Around two in the morning several neighbors "heard what they now know was the explosion; one or two got up, looked out on to the street, and, seeing nothing unusual . . . they again retired." The burglars went to George Colby's barn, where they stole his "most valuable" horse and a wagon. At 5 a.m., discovering his horse gone, Colby took off in pursuit. "Meanwhile the telephone had been kept busy" notifying other towns to be on the lookout. Colby followed the tracks, "which were quite plain," to West Peterborough, where the robbers had thoughtfully hitched his horse behind a barn. Word reached Peterborough a half-hour late; "Three strange men" were seen boarding the first train to Winchendon. They were never caught.

On May 25, 1913, one month after his 31st birthday, Clinton gave up diary keeping. He had not missed a beat, or hardly a temperature, for fifteen years. With his mother, he moved out of town to a farm. He and his partner had folded their phone business by 1910 and split the cash on hand ($86). But Clinton still believed in telephones; at his new poultry farm he put a phone in the brooder house.

Clinton and his mother later moved to Keene, a small city some twenty miles away. Late in his thirties, he married "a girl from Gilsum," Helen Leach, and had two sons. He worked at the Keene post office, eventually becoming the chief clerk. Steadiness ran in the family. His brother, Everrett, served Antrim as a mailman on an R.F.D. route for forty years. Everett's wife, Ethel, was the town's librarian for twenty-five years.

Clinton Preston Davis' gathering of days would have gone to dust in an attic or a barn, but his son Kermit found the diaries and typed them up. "Even as I gently turned and transcribed the pages of these ancient diaries," Kermit says, "numerous leaves disintegrated beneath my touch, falling in flakes from their bindings." Some years have vanished. (1903, 1908, 1910, and 1911.)

The last time Kermit saw his father and grandmother was in their home in Keene. "It was in late November 1943. I turned and waved as I walked to the train, on my way to Army service overseas. When I returned in 1946, they had both passed away."

Clarence Derby's USA

I. "Everything for Everybody"

The McGilvray Room is a locked, air-conditioned room upstairs from the reference section in the town library of Peterborough, New Hampshire. Patrons have to sign in at the circulation desk to get the key. I had not been there for years, so I did what I usually do when I'm admitted to special collections: I roamed the shelves, opening books—on some shelves nearly every book. I looked at gazetteers, almanacs, census records, laws, town histories, old railroad annual reports, bits of local school lore, chamber of commerce brochures. This was what I was doing when I came across six blue loose-leaf binders and one red binder on a low shelf to the right of the door.

I flipped through the pages of the first binder. Each page is a collage: advertising, receipts, invoices, accounting, photos, and a short typed commentary. It's like looking through the drawers of an old rolltop desk. The title for these 425 pages is *Goodnows, Goodnow & Derby, Pictures, Comments, Advertising. By Clarence Derby. Written 1989–90*. But as I read the book I came to think of it as *Clarence Derby's USA*. In his retirement, sitting at his kitchen table, Clarence Derby had assembled the book about his family's Peterborough department store. He had taken an old form, the merchant's daybook, the diary of commerce, and made it new. It is an uncanny history of the ordinary. In a few loose-leaf binders Clarence has captured things in motion—all the things that people handled daily that defined daily life and then vanished. It's like a sequence of 19th-century motion-study photographs—the horse galloping, the man leaping, the common goods of trade passed from hand to hand. For more than a hundred years it all flowed through Derby's. In this biography of commerce, this *roman-fleuve*, Clarence has given commerce dignity. This is more than "creative destruction," the economic upheaval that leaves us bewildered. *Clarence Derby's USA* is a documentary about the soul of a store.

I set aside my initial research errand and sat there entranced with *Volume 1, Part 1: 1882–1929.*

"There is no attempt to make this book an authentic history," Clarence begins. "Possibly twenty-five years ago I started accumulating these stories and recording them. My father, John Derby, gave me some of these facts.

"At the age of ten or earlier I sometimes went to the store directly from school to do menial or small jobs a ten-year-old could do. Putting up potatoes or sugar, packing eggs were a few of the jobs I did to earn a little money besides dipping into the candy or cookie departments when no one was looking. My name is on the payroll books of 1917 as receiving twenty-five cents per week. . . . This was the first payroll I was on and the last was in 1979, 62 years later. I never worked or earned any money except at this store and I enjoyed the work very much."

Clarence had two older brothers, Robert and Carl. Their father, John, had started working in the store at age nineteen. He had walked twenty-five miles from his family's farm hoping to get a job. He was hired as clerk in 1892 for a yearly salary of $100 plus room and board. This was the customary apprenticeship. Seven years later he was invited to buy a quarter interest in the business, which was then renamed Goodnow & Derby. ("Everything for Everybody. Goodnow & Derby.") With his brother, George, he bought the business by 1907. They did well, building a chain of seven additional country stores in surrounding towns. Robert went off to Dartmouth, Carl and Clarence to the University of New Hampshire. Robert came home to manage a bookstore around the corner and Carl to help his father manage the store.

In late August 1929 Clarence had packed his trunk to go back for his last year of college when his father had a stroke. He decided to stay to help his brother Carl run the store until the January semester. His father did not get better, so he put off his return to the start of the next school year in September. "Never did make it back for my final year," he said. Clarence would work eleven years before taking his first vacation.

On the eve of the Great Depression Goodnow & Derby was a country store selling many goods the way they had been sold since the Civil War. In the windowless basement, with its cobwebbed low ceilings, dirt floor, and rough stone walls, they stored potatoes and cabbage in bulk, wooden barrels of pickles, vinegar, and molasses, and large tanks of linseed oil and turpentine.

"Customers would bring in their stone jugs for molasses," Clarence recalled. "Of course you could not see how much you had in the jug when filling it. The molasses was cranked out of the wooden barrel and for each eight turns a quart would go into the jug. Thirty-two turns would fill a gallon jug and not run it over. The jug neck was small and if you cranked too fast the jug would overflow and make a sticky mess." Vinegar jugs were made of glass and were easier to fill.

Coffee came in burlap bags. "We used to grind coffee from the bean according to our customers' wishes, fine, medium or coarse. . . . The A&P manager told me once how he would put the bags of coffee under the sink so they would absorb moisture and then he could get more coffee from the bag. We never did this."

Eggs, produce, and some meat came from local farms; everything else came in on the railroad and was unloaded with one of the store's horse-drawn wagons. Their dry-goods supplier was in New York City, which was a lot farther from New Hampshire than it is today. There were no deliveries by truck. Each dish towel, Crayola, and bobby pin had to be sent by steamship east to Boston and then loaded on the Boston & Maine Railroad to finish the trip north and west.

Groceries were delivered to the store's customers by horse and wagon. Two men called on houses in the morning, taking orders that would be delivered that afternoon. "Telephones at this time were not common in all homes and the salesman could sell more goods by a personal call," Clarence said. Sleighs were used in the winter. In the early 1920s, autos were put up on blocks and covered under sheets from the first of November until "the snow was gone and the frost was out of the ground." A horse-pulled snow roller kept the streets open. "It was impossible to get out of town except by train."

Goodnow & Derby was still delivering groceries by horse and wagon in the early 1930s, though many customers now had cars and came to the store. The deliveryman, Jim Allen, could not drive a truck. He kept the horse and wagon at his house.

In the store, clerks waited on all customers, picking and packing their orders. All food came in bulk. The store's interior was a series of counters, cabinets, drawers, and big bins with roll tops. Rows of drawers built into the wall held spices and small grocery items. The bins held bulk cereals, sugar, and beans. Candy and tobacco were in glass cases.

They also sold dynamite (to blast stubborn New Hampshire granite), twenty-five cents a stick. "The sticks would come packed in a wooden box packed with a little sawdust. The box would be one foot high by two feet by two feet. We usually bought them four boxes at a time. They would come alone in a freight car, safely secured in the middle of the car. Used to keep this in the warehouse. I remember moving boxes of the stuff and getting it for customers and it seemed to me my knees were like rubber and going to collapse. Did not like doing this at all."

꙰

Before his stroke, John had planned to convert the grocery department in all his stores to self-service, to the kind of market we know today. He had joined the Independent Grocers Alliance (IGA). This was going to be a big break with the past; Goodnow & Derby would be a long way from the store John first knew in 1892. Carl and Clarence decided to go ahead with the remodeling.

The brothers began tearing out cabinets and drawers. "We found that mice had lived there for years and left their trademarks. It really was a very dirty and messy job. . . . Both drawers and bins had been there for years and probably were handmade." Out they went. Carpenters built new wooden shelves. "The open shelving was a big change from clerk service and our help was not entirely satisfied." It was Peterborough's first self-service grocery.

"All merchandise would come packaged in the future and only shelves were needed. We personally painted them a cream color and the edges were dark blue. These were the official IGA colors and we used the same colors on the shelves all over the store. Carl and I did the painting. All this was completed and we opened in the middle of October 1929, about the time the stock market crashed."

Hard times. Sales plummeted. From 1930 to 1933 their sales were down by nearly half. They had to stop offering credit, which in good times was as much as eighty percent of their sales. The store was cash only. "Customers were not paying their accounts. Times were that bad," said Clarence. In West Peterborough "the White Mill was running very short hours and some days not at all. No one was earning enough to live on or pay their bills." The town's Overseer of the Poor paid their grocery bills. Things got worse. The Derby's warehouse burned down in 1931. Peterborough was hit by a flood in 1936 and was flooded again two years later by the devastating 1938 hurricane. The first flood raced through the store's foundation, water coming into the cellar faster than it could escape. Clarence, Carl, and a handyman stayed in the store all night, trying to move the water out. If the waters hadn't receded in the morning, the front of the building may have collapsed, said Clarence. The hurricane flooded the basement again (five feet deep) and part of the first floor (eightteen inches deep). (Flood insurance was unheard of.) The wind tore off half the tin roof. Around the corner, the town was in flames. Clarence took the account books and fled. Shingles blew off roofs; a tree shattered right in front of him. He could go no farther; cradling the account books, he sat down on the steps of a house. He stayed the night with a neighbor.

All this happens in *Volume 1, Part 2: 1930–39* and you might expect it to be grim reading. But it's not. Even though Clarence is writing fifty years later, he still manages to convey the bumptious flexibility of a young man starting out in the world. "Most everything we did was a big event," he writes. I'm struck by Clarence's easygoing manner, his enjoyment of trade, and his willingness to learn and to change his business. He uses the word *enjoy* to describe sales and sales meetings. When things go wrong—a product doesn't sell, a customer complains or sues or steals, an employee steals or a salesman cheats them, he notes it as a lesson and moves on. In this commercial memoir, at least, he seems incapable of holding a grudge or regret. He remembers and moves on.

He even forgives the IRS. After they were audited for the first time—"He gave us a real hard time"—Clarence takes it as a "very good lesson." They hired professional accountants.

There were other lessons, too. "Sometime in my early years of helping to manage the store, I learned a good lesson cheap. A man came in and told us he had some fine potatoes at a good price. Probably this might have been in the spring when they were hard to get or expensive. He opened up a bag of them and they looked very good for the price he was asking. We told him that we would take several bags like the sample. He brought them in and we paid cash. When we opened the other bags, they were small and had sprouted badly. This man was a lot smarter than we were at the time. This was a very good lesson and experience."

He also uses the word *satisfied.* Clarence was paid $10 a week in 1933. His recently married brother was given a raise to $15 a week. "I was living at home and was satisfied." This word—*satisfied*—reoccurs in *Clarence Derby's USA*. It's an old-fashioned, calming word. Advertisements used to promise that customers would be satisfied. Goodnow & Derby had painted the promise on the side of their store: "Peterborough's Satisfactory Shopping Place." In this way Clarence is an old-fashioned merchant. He's not creating desires, but filling needs with "ordinary merchandise."

The Derbys had the right mix of experience and youth to survive the Depression. Their father, though retired, came to the store almost daily to confer with his sons. This mix was lacking in their other stores and they often scrambled to cover for a delinquent manager. It was a hands-on business in the way that old ships required many hands. By 1937 they had closed the other stores and incorporated the remaining store in Peterborough as Derby's.

Clarence could tell in a glance who was a bad merchant. He doesn't dwell on it, but all around Derby's, merchants come and go: the grocer who was understocked and ran out the back door to buy from Derby's ("We did not mind."); the clothier whose store was a jumble; the cook who never ordered enough meat and was always waking up Carl, who lived over the store. These short mentions are often followed by the words: "He went out of business."

After Clarence adds up the swooning sales figures for the Depression decade, he writes, "Sometimes I feel it was remarkable we came through the period."

They did more than just hang on. They kept changing the store. "Groceries, meats, fruits and vegetables really do not mix well with dry goods, notions and hardware in any retail establishment," said Clarence. In 1937 they moved the food from the main floor to the back, clearing "2,100 square feet to devote to notions, stationery, candy, toiletries, women's hosiery and underwear, infantwear, hardware and housewares. It was a layout on one floor no store in Peterborough had ever had and an assortment of merchandise the citizens of Peterborough needed. We were very glad to furnish it.

"This was one of the first big changes we made in the layout of the store. It seems as though we changed continually." We tend to think of old stores nostalgically. We have a frozen-clock notion of commerce, fixing on the old days of penny candy or some other bygone instant. But the Derby's story is all change—it's a continuous performance.

They sent out a mimeographed sheet to customers showing the new floor plan. Clarence had photos taken, something he did each time they remodeled. The local weekly, *The Peterborough Transcript*, was impressed. "Entering the store, one's first thought is that he is in a modern 5-, 10-, and 25-cent store. . . . New shelves and gaily painted counters give a colorful tone to this new department."

In the 1930s they also added a meat department, a furniture department with two showrooms, women's dresses, and accessories. They got a better hardware supplier. They stopped selling lumber and 3.2 beer. "Looking back on this beer episode, it was not anything we should have done. One of our clerks was a deacon of the Congregational Church and another was a relative of mine and he was terribly against drinks of this type."

They were late adopting one innovation: frozen food. "We made a mistake not getting Birds Eye from the very first." Another store in town had taken it on. Even so, people were slow to try Birds Eye's Frosted Foods. Refrigerators didn't have freezer compartments and no stores had display freezers. "There would have to be a lot of selling the idea of frozen foods for it to be successful."

There were other new products. "I remember very well the salesman who introduced us to selling dog food in a can. The brand was Ken-L- Ration. The salesman would open a can of the dog food in the store and take a few bites. This would prove to us and our customers that Ken-L-Ration was OK and would not make your dog sick. I never ate any of it with him however."

Lists are a big part of *Clarence Derby's USA*. They are one of the timekeeping pieces. Here's one: "A list of items that were stocked by most country stores in the 1930s. They were ordinary items then, but living has changed and most of these items have disappeared from most ordinary stores." A few items from Clarence's list, with the year they were sold at Derby's:

1931	Men's long leg underwear	.79
1931	Drive calks (used on horse shoes)	.05
1933	Kerosene cook stoves	
	(2 burner)	$13.95
	(3 burner)	$17.95
	(4 burner)	$21.95 (4 b.)
1933	Voss Wringer Washer *A novelty at the time.*	$49.95
1933	Hay rake teeth	.10 dozen
1933	Hoe handles	.25
1933	Glass chimneys for lamps	.15 for 2
1935	Horse blankets	$5.00
1936	Pure silk full-fashion hosiery	.69
1937	Antifreeze for autos	.75 gal.
1939	Hand lawn mowers	$9.95

∞

"About this year, 1935, the World Series was a subway series in New York City. Brooklyn for the National League and New York for the American League. Because we did so much business with Butler Brothers in New York City I asked them to get two seats for the Sunday game that was in Yankee Stadium. Scott Appleton, our meat man, was a baseball fan and I asked him to go with me.

"We started from Peterborough at five a.m. and arrived in New York City in plenty of time to find our seats. There were many thousands of fans between us and home plate. All the fans seemed to be smoking and we could not see very much. One of the players hit a home run and we didn't see or know it happened. This was the only World Series I ever had a chance to see and it was worth it."

II. An American Clock

Carl Derby died suddenly in January 1942, after an operation, leaving Clarence to run the family business. "While talking with my father after Carl's death, he gave me some of the best advice anyone could get. He told me I should always manage the store easily and enjoy the process. I did this for the next 38 years, following his advice. It was always a pleasure owning and operating Derby's."

This occurs at the beginning of *Volume 2, 1940–1959*. A new book with new hardships: The war years, shortages, rationing. Pearl Harbor had been attacked the month before his brother died. Clarence was at the Unitarian Parish Hall "putting on an oyster stew supper for the Layman's League." They kept the radio on, listening to the news from Hawaii.

Clarence had $10,000 from his brother's life-insurance policy and decided to invest the money in Derby's. The previous year they had expanded the grocery department once more; now it was time to update the rest of the store. He ordered new fixtures and a new storefront from a company in Nebraska. Four men cut up the old shelves and displays with big crosscut saws and dumped the parts in the alley. The store was closed for a week and reopened for its 60th anniversary. "Come in Saturday and see The . . . Country Store 'Gone Modern,'" Clarence's wife, Charlotte, wrote in an advertisement. "We are proud to have been Peterborough's General Store for sixty years, but we'd like to be considered progressive." Four thousand people turned out that Saturday, an impressive turnout for a town of only 2,500. The new, modern storefront displayed antiques from a local museum of Americana: a Penny Farthing bicycle, a baby carriage, a Victrola, gowns and dresses from the 1880s on mannequins. It was a pageant of progress.

The new storefront was Art Deco, though by 1942 this modern touch was already dated. Art Deco took its name from a 1925 Paris exposition and reached its peak in the United States in the early 1930s as the assured style of skyscrapers such as the Chrysler Building, Rockefeller Center, and the Empire State Building. In 1942 Peterborough went modern with a delivery from Nebraska.

In an editorial, *The Peterborough Transcript* praised Derby's for exhibiting "one outstanding and common characteristic, frequently lacking in the direction of many of our older establishments, that of keeping a keen eye on the future and being quick to take action. . . . They haven't waited to be forced to either adjust or quit, but have kept a step or two ahead of the procession by making decisions to meet the demands of the moment and never forgetting that . . . revolutionary changes come about these days in a matter of hours, rather than weeks or months. . . . Their store is a credit to Peterborough . . . the Derbys have never forgotten their civic responsibilities."

Clarence has pages of black-and-white photos showing the store before and after its transformation: the main floor looking toward the front, and looking toward the rear, and the second floor women's department. He believed in remodeling.

I have spent a long time peering into these small before-and-after photos, yet I confess that if the order were reshuffled I would be unable to tell. I feel bad about this because Clarence was so proud of his remodeling, but—before or after—the store just seems jammed from floor to ceiling in a way that modern stores are not. Most of us don't shop at toe-level anymore, except in old hardware stores, which are like a *Where's Waldo* treasure hunt for a faucet washer. (There's a hardware store near me in an old wooden building with narrow aisles packed with stuff, every inch is used. It's like being inside a toolbox.)

To the contemporary shopper, Derby's would seem to be a narrow tunnel with a low ceiling supported by a forest of poles. Old mercantile space was a long shoebox, as were old theaters and urban row houses. Frontage cost you; your lot jostled for a slice of the street.

Modern retail space, schools, and some theaters are "big boxes." They are horizontal space, the grid of the West transposed to the supermarket. We come in the door and we expect roaming space. We want an interstate freeway experience instead of the small streets of downtown. In the modern superstore you can swing through an aerobics workout. Not in Derby's. So I will have to take Clarence Derby's word when he says of the before-and-after photos: Look at the improvements. It still seems jammed.

Clarence found the wartime shortages and regulations frustrating. He had many orders rejected: "Due to shortage we are canceling your order." "Due to shortage we are substituting your order." "Out of stock. Please reorder." "Can not supply." "Cancelled. Not made any longer." Or they would send what they had on hand, "allotment merchandise." "Some of it was just plain junk," said Clarence.

"Because of the shortages in so much merchandise there was a lot of bickering between our customers and clerks as to whether we had the merchandise, and if we did, who was supposed to be able to buy it. Customers would watch for the trucks that brought these scarce items to the store and then come swarming in to get their share. Cigarettes, butter, oleo, lard, and meats were the very scarce and hard-to-get items. They would stand in line and when we would run out they did not believe us. There never was enough of some things to satisfy all the customers. We used to hide some of the things under the counters and give to our loyal customers."

Metal was scarce: There were wooden toys, pails, jewelry, frameless lampshades, and since there was no nickel plating, knitting needles, safety pins, bicycles, and alarm clocks were all black. The production of appliances, radios, cars, and 600 other types of consumer goods was suspended. Leather was also scarce and shoes "were made with rubber soles that had a lot of carbon in them and would mark the floors badly." The synthetic elastic in underwear, garters, and suspenders did not have "much stretch." There were no silk stockings. Derby's traded with other stores, swapping nylon stockings for hardware, buying flashlight batteries ("never could get as many as we wanted"), lunchboxes, padlocks, combs, eyeglasses, men's pants. They bought "black-market beef" from local farms.

There were five ration categories. Customers had blue stamps for canned fruit and vegetables, dried beans, baby foods, soups, some jams and jellies; red stamps for meat, fat, butter, cheese, and canned fish; and stamps for sugar, coffee, and shoes. Derby's was required to deposit these ration points in special bank accounts and draw rationing checks to send to their suppliers. Somehow it was all supposed to add up: the points, the checks, the store's inventory, and taxes paid. The Home Front required the small business owner to file a Niagara of paperwork. Clarence had to fill out 200 pages of detailed inventories for the Office of Price Administration (OPA) to show that he was complying with the price ceilings. The forms look daunting. Each invoice had to be stamped with an assigned item number, category number, rule number, net cost, mark-up percentage, and maximum OPA selling price. "We did the best we could," Clarence said. One OPA inspector claimed that he was short on shoe rationing coupons. Clarence spent all day in court and although he proved that he had the right number of coupons, the judge ordered him not to sell rationed shoes for one week. Shoe rationing ended within a month.

Even with his appearance in a "kangaroo court" and other OPA inspections, Clarence judged the regulators to be "very demanding but, on the whole, I believe it was rather effective."

"Looking back over these invoices and records, the struggle from this distance in time seems to have been greater than it actually was between 1942 and 1946. One WWII veteran, who chanced to see this record, exclaimed he was glad he was in the service! I really could not agree with him."

Clarence's wife, Charlotte, added "Favorite Recipes of Peterborough Women" to their newspaper ads to help cooks make the best use of their rationing points. On May 4, 1944, Derby's Super Market for Everyday Low Prices offered "Reception Salad." "This recipe is a little hard on ration points, but now that reductions have been made on so many canned foods, you will probably have enough points to splurge a little for your most special company.

"Try it when 'the girls' come in for the evening:

1 pkg. lemon gelatine
Juice from one large can
crushed pineapple
Crushed pineapple from the can
2 cream cheese mashed with
1 small can pimentos

½ cup celery cut fine
⅔ cup walnut meats
½ pt. cream, whipped
⅛ tsp. salt

Mix lemon gelatine with pineapple juice, which has been boiled. When mixture begins to jell, add other ingredients in order given, and allow to stand in mold or individual molds until set. Serve on crisp lettuce. About 10 servings."

∞

Nineteen forty-six was a banner year. The war was over; returning veterans, who had grown up in the Depression, were eager to get on with their lives. Factories resumed production of appliances and radios. "For about the first six months of 1946 we could sell almost any brand of appliance within a very few days." They delivered six refrigerators in one day. "At the time we had only one truck and the delivery men certainly had to hustle." Mostly the appliances came in one or two at a time. There was a waiting list. They tried to serve the veterans first. The rush for refrigerators, washers, ranges, and radios lasted about a year, boosting Derby's' profits by seventy percent. "Nineteen forty-six was an exceptional year and it was very satisfying. It was never duplicated, sorry to say."

Selling appliances was new for Derby's. They experimented "with any merchandise that would bring in sales," said Clarence. "We stocked hearing aids, eyeglasses, sewing machines, wallpaper, a gift department, floor furnaces, kerosene heaters and stoves. Most of these items were unsuccessful and were dropped." They also stocked many things for their customers' convenience. "Many items were not in the other stores and we considered it an obligation to have this material available locally . . . window glass in all sizes; rifles, shotguns, and ammunition; paint, enamel, and varnish; lamp shades, window shades; linoleum by the yard, with installation service; Congoleum rugs in all sizes; baby furniture and carriages; wheelbarrows, lawn mowers, grass seed, and fertilizers; fish poles and fishing equipment; rubbers and rubber boots." Derby's advertised as a department store with "37 complete departments." (It sounded like Heinz's 57 Varieties, Clarence said.)

Sales had started to grow in the last years of the war. Clarence expanded the store again, reclaiming the cellar where he had begun in the business filling molasses jugs. To lower the floor a foot, many large boulders were drilled into pieces and removed—there was stone dust all over the store. The walls were smoothed over and lighting added. The first 1,000 square feet were ready for Christmas toys in 1945—cheap toys made of paper, wood, and plastic because of wartime shortages. The other half of the cellar was dug out and opened in the following two years. Derby's was now 10,000 square feet, "the largest store in the Monadnock Region, carrying one of the most diversified lines of any store in the state."

But their share of the local grocery business was decreasing; chain stores had come to Peterborough. In 1947 Clarence made the difficult decision to end 65 years of selling groceries. During the Depression groceries had accounted for more than 50 percent of their business, but Derby's could make more money selling appliances and furniture. (There was a 20 percent mark-up on foods, but a 35 percent mark-up on other merchandise.) In two years Derby's made up what they had lost in food sales. Hardware, housewares, and toys were selling well and expanded greatly in the next 30 years. "The decision to eliminate foods was absolutely correct," he said.

That year Clarence's father died. Though he had lost his advisor, he was supported by long-time employees and by his wife. Clarence and Charlotte had two sons: John, born in 1941, and Charles, in 1944. They would grow up and join him in the business, but already they were changing Derby's. "We were made aware of the amount of clothing, toys, furniture, etc., young parents have to buy their children. At the time our stocks for young customers were inadequate. Because we had to purchase for our children, we learned by experience what other parents were buying and added these items to our inventory.

"Could it be possible these two boys paid for themselves?"

Prosperity and shortages brought inflation. Clarence worked through the invoices from his grocery supplier for 1940–47 to figure the rate of inflation. Some sample items:

	1940	1947
Quaker Oats, lg. pkg. (case of 12)	1.69	2.90
Campbell's Tomato Soup (case of 48)	3.49	4.39
Sugar (carton of 12, 5-lb. bags)	3.00	5.32
Maxwell House Coffee (case of 12)	2.82	5.56
Oysters (gallon)	1.30	5.85
Butter (1 lb.)	.24	.81

In seven years, the price of grocery items in his survey increased seventy percent.

After years of sacrifice in depression and war, merchants and manufacturers were in a holiday mood. Two advertisements:

July 24, 1947 —

Derby's Headquarters For Everything Electrical...
You won't believe your eyes
when you see the new
AUTOMAGIC
THOR GLADIRON!

Women said the Thor Gladiron couldn't be improved—but wait 'till you see the new Automagic Gladiron! It takes even the *hand-work* out of ironing—you'll use your hands only for guiding clothes through the famous Gladiron roll. Coming soon—watch for it!

It will pay for itself in a short time
Only $99.50
Easy Budget Terms at Derby's

February 12, 1948—

Shop at Derby's in 1948. The values are there. Nationally known brands available. Service is good. Clerks are pleasant. All under one roof.

Clarence loved sales. He loved the 9 Cent Sales they held in the 1930s. Among other 9-cent items, Derby's sold an 18-cent galvanized pail for 9 cents. "Our customers knew a bargain and would line up to buy the pails. It was fun to see the customers go for such a bargain." He loved the rug remnant sales they ran starting in 1968. People lined up early and Clarence went down the line finding out where they came from and handing out store souvenirs. Some people asked to camp out in the parking lot (although no one ever did).

In 1943 he hired Guy Little, an assistant manager with a flair for sales. Clarence had been running the business alone since his brother's death and "the job was too much for one person." Little wrote ads like this one for the week before July 4, 1954: "Derby's 72nd Anniversary and Big Fireworks Show. We're Shooting the Works!! . . . Red Hot Buys . . . Bedding Bombshells . . . We're Exploding Chair Prices." On the 4th Derby's had free fireworks in the town park, sponsored by some manufacturers who displayed their logos in fireworks: Norge, Zenith, Westinghouse, Ball Band, and others. Little worked at Derby's for the next thirty-five years. "He was one hundred percent responsible for the growth in hardware, TV, and appliances that eventually became fifty percent of our business," Clarence said.

Derby's first big post-war sale in 1949 was so busy that for the second sale a few months later, Clarence hired a police officer to keep order in the crowded parking lot. He also hired a photographer. In one photo a clerk is holding up a toaster as people crowd in. It's a scene with the high spirits of old open-air bazaars. These sales are just like Old Home Day, said one customer; you meet all your friends.

Each sale had a theme. On one page Clarence lists 60 different sale names: Back Door Sale, Clerks' Sale, Hog Wild Sale, 1 Minute Sale, 4 Hour Sale, 5 Hour Sale, 23 Hour Sale, Derby Days, O'Derby Days (St. Patrick's Day), Heat Wave of Values, Camp and Cottage Sale, Krazy Days Sale, Balloon Sale, Cat-Dog Sale, Locked In Sale, Mis Match Sale, Remodeling Sale, Out They Go Sale, Biggest Discount Sale, Let's Go to Derby's First Sale. . . .

Clarence and Guy were game to try almost anything. They had sales in which they reduced the price of a bedroom set five dollars an hour until someone bought it and sales where they marked down just one piece of furniture, and opened the doors to a land rush as people raced to be the first to claim a chair by sitting on it. They advertised that Derby's would take Christmas present returns from any store: "So . . . You Got A Gift You Didn't Want, eh? Derby's Will Exchange It!" A few neckties came in, but that was about it.

For the Locked In Sale, Derby's salesmen kept the furniture warehouse open for thirty hours. The salesmen were photographed in homemade prison stripes, with their hands up as Peterborough's police chief pointed his finger, gun-like, at them. For the Balloon Sale, balloons were marked with reductions from ten to fifty percent. After making a purchase, a customer took a balloon down from overhead. "Sorry to say there was some shifty work done by some customers in trying to find the balloon with the largest percentage," Clarence said.

"Derby's was an aggressive retailer," recalled Paul Cummings, the senior publisher of *The Peterborough Transcript*. By that I think he meant that Derby's really wanted to sell you something and worked to please you. Many other Yankee merchants thought they had done enough just by showing up and opening the store. They had a few things for sale. If that was what you wanted, good. If it wasn't, you should make do. In any case, they weren't going to make a big noise. Clarence spent about two percent of his yearly sales income on advertising. He made a big noise.

He was a curator, the town's representative in the marketplace. People relied on him to get a better-quality item. He studied the goods in higher-end stores on trips to Boston and New York City. With his sales staff, he made three trips a year to find good closeout items for sales. ("Mammoth Colossal Closeout.") After the sales he marked the ads to see what really sold. There are many pages of ads in *Clarence Derby's USA*, each item marked with the number sold or simply: good, fair, or poor.

Derby's sales were supported by national companies building their brands. They paid for advertising and sent out salespeople to put on shows. Westinghouse sponsored cooking lessons: The Westinghouse All-Electric Mystery Show. (Hawaiian Pork Chops, Hamburgers Deluxe, Orange Pudding, Pecan Pie.) On a special demonstration day Derby's advertised that Mr. Sunbeam would give you a shave with a Super Sunbeam Shaver, Mr. Lewyt would show the new Lewyt Vacuum cleaner, Mr. Cory would serve coffee, Miss Thor would iron, and Miss Westinghouse would cook a full Thanksgiving dinner in a Westinghouse roaster oven.

Sometimes the show spilled out the front door. Derby's introduced a new floor covering, "Floorever," by installing a six-foot-wide piece from the front door across the street to the post office. An elephant—followed by a Derby's employee with a broom and a dustpan—was brought in to walk across the "Floorever."

The Derby's sales and promotions were a mix of the slick and the homegrown, the corporate and the small town. To introduce freezers at the annual summer street fair, the store held a contest to guess the weight of a pig. (Three hundred and seventy-five pounds—but this, too, was a guess. They had no scale to weigh the pig.) The winner would take home the pig, butchered, and a new freezer to put it in. But "Rosebud" apparently went home in one piece and was known around Peterborough for several years. Another year, Derby's auctioned off a Shetland pony named, in a contest, "Buckets." Customers bid with "Derby Bucks" they had earned with purchases. The Derby Bucks were good only at the auction, setting in motion a kind of Confederate currency. As each of the items leading up to the pony was auctioned, the Bucks became wildly inflated and then were instantly worthless. At another fair in the park, the challenge was to guess how many kernels of cracked corn a caged rooster would eat. Everyone lost track and the rooster flew off into the Nubanusit River—"he sailed over the dam just like a small boat"—before being rescued.

One promotion was locally famous but much regretted by Clarence. In 1955 his furniture manager had signed up a model to demonstrate a Sealy mattress and box spring in the front window.

"Considerable advertising in the usual Derby fashion announced the mattress show," *Transcript* publisher Paul Cummings recalled. The audience arrived early, at one point almost blocking the street. "About mid-morning . . . with the crowd growing anxious . . . a scantily clad female appeared on the scene and slipped into her bedstead.

"A howl went up from the sidewalk throng when, from a distance, the woman looked to be attired only in a see-through nightgown, or that was the illusion she created. Beneath the lingerie, it was soon apparent she was encased in a flesh-colored body suit, which contributed further to the 'oohs' and 'aahs' of onlookers.

"The demonstration, to put this in its proper perspective, was brief. Within minutes, three or four at the most, the lady leaped out of the bed, ducked behind a screen, and was on her way out of town.

"'No hussy, me,' the salesgirl was said to have exclaimed in an angry voice to Mrs. Derby as she bolted from the store."

Charlotte was not pleased. The woman in the window, said Cummings, "came close to causing a crisis in the Derby household." In his note above Cummings' recollection, Clarence said, "One of our managers was the responsible person and probably I did not know just what the deal was."

Derby's store was an American clock. In the post-war years changes arrived in Peterborough, at Derby's, right on time, as if ordered by a social historian: the first television, the first color television, the first shopping center. You can chart the rise of the great consumer society in this one country store turned five-and-dime turned department store. Clarence, who began in the cellar packing potatoes and filling jugs of vinegar, was now selling Philco televisions.

When the first televisions arrived in 1948 there was almost nothing to see, but people were so eager to have one that Derby's sold homemade antennas to pull in the few Boston stations. He hired a TV repairman and quickly added a second. Derby's sold the first color television in the Monadnock region in 1956, even though, again, almost all shows were still broadcast in black and white.

In 1957 Derby's advertised itself as a "SHOPPING CENTER"—all capital letters—with plenty of "convenient parking." The next year, on the "Grove St. Extension," Peterborough's first, small shopping center opened and called itself a "shopping village." The shopping center's promoters wanted Derby's as a tenant, but Clarence decided to stay put; the previous year he had remodeled and expanded the store. For the 75th Diamond Jubilee anniversary, the Art Deco storefront was replaced with a new front that is classic 1950s: Derby's in script on a façade that was raked forward in the spirit of the Detroit tail-fin era. Again Derby's celebrated its anniversary and the "New 1957 Look!" with antiques in the window and special sales.

Facing a short recession, and the new shopping center, Clarence prepared a special "bulletin" for his staff: "Let's all pull together," he urged, and "make better friends of our customers." The store prospered through the 1960s. By 1969 Derby's covered 22,500 square feet in four buildings around a sixty-car parking lot, "Derby Square." The store had the majority of the television and appliance business for fifteen miles around, and for years it was the first and only furniture store in town. Clarence had also opened three branch stores.

Derby's best years, Clarence said, were 1957 to 1969—also some of the best years for the U.S. economy.

III. "Some Kid Stole a Hat"

Volume 3, 1960 to 1969, begins quietly. This is not the quick, jump-cut history of Civil Rights protests, campus sit-ins, and urban riots that has become the standard Sixties documentary. At first look, the world at 30 Grove Street is a seamless whole, unshaken and expanding since the veterans returned and Clarence could sell any appliance he could get. In Peterborough it seems to be the 1950s with the addition of color TV. Derby's sale ads look the same as they did in the 1950s; the employees dress the same. The interior photos seem closer to the early 1950s than to the Summer of Love or the summer of *Steal This Book*. But as *Volume 3* progresses, the tone changes slightly as new events seep in: "Two kids caught stealing. Gave them what for." "I refused credit to a person who became very mad." "Mrs. R___ mad about TV service charge; G___ M___ provoked at furniture salesmen."

In *Volume 3*, Clarence reveals what I should have suspected long ago: He was a devout diary keeper. Here he types out some of his entries, each day noted in a sentence or two. I recognize the form—the terse, telegraphic daybook of labor. I don't know why I should find this surprising; he kept many lists. Clarence kept track. He was a timekeeper of commerce. That's one reason why he succeeded: He tracked what sold and what didn't; what it cost to advertise; how fast stock turned over; and, in his "Beat Yesterday" book, how sales compared on the same day a year prior.

In November 1963 he wrote this in his journal:

1 Someone attached E___ K___ 's pay. He was a serviceman. Some kid stole a hat.

6 Manchester to buy Cinderella dresses with Marion Griswold.
7 Went to Newport with Roy Robbins about a new manager.
20 Boston to Wellington Sears for special merchandise.
22 President Kennedy assassinated and closed store.
25 Kennedy funeral. Closed all day.

A kid steals a hat. Clarence goes to Manchester to buy Cinderella dresses. The president is murdered. We're doing the small things and then there's an earthquake. This is how most of us experience headline news. Where were you when . . . ? we ask each other. Where were you when Kennedy was shot? The lights went out on the East Coast? The shuttle exploded? The planes hit the towers?

In the first collection of essays about the attacks of 9-11, the writers had to tell everyone where they were when they heard the news: I was here, I was standing there, I was doing this. I looked out of where I was and this is what I saw—my breath, my hand, my love. And off on a wire and a wave comes the world and its news. There's always this comparison—our lives and the big event, as if two parallel universes had opened to each other at the moment of calamity. Two clocks are revealed to be ticking side by side: The clock of the Empire and the clock of our lives, borne along on the current. I was living my day. I was on my way to Manchester to buy a Cinderella dress.

I was once briefly involved in a local Amnesty International chapter that was forming to petition governments to release political prisoners. We were packed full of ourselves. Our letters would free prisoners. We were working to right the world. Coming in to the library where we met, we passed a roomful of people—thirty or forty—happily playing bridge. *Playing bridge while the world burned.* We didn't have to take a vote to commend ourselves on our virtue.

But why did we want to free the poor prisoners in other countries? Why? So they would be free to pass the time, make a thousand meals for their families, sit in the pub, play bridge. So they would be free to buy their daughters Cinderella dresses. We live in the mundane. You can dismiss daily life as trivial, or you can welcome its simple joys.

Mundane. Done again. Thousands upon thousands of items flowed out of Derby's. Nail clippers, thumbtacks, underwear, toothpaste, shoes, Cinderella dresses. Each mundane; each also a devotion.

Clarence Derby knew this. He was a curator of this kinetic museum. He looked after his customers—his neighbors—by procuring the best goods he could find. "We had a subconscious feeling of the way Peterborough wanted this store to be managed," he said. "We gave our best to do this always."

Another list. On the 100th anniversary of Derby's in 1982, Clarence totaled up the number of years his employees had worked for him. It is startling in this era of minimum-wage slavery in big-box stores to see how many people made a decent living for decades at one family-owned department store:

Lester Cockburn	15 years
Sandra Cleary	20
David Crooker	36
Carl Derby	15
Charles Derby	20
Charlotte Derby	43 (as an officer)
Clarence Derby	50
John Derby II	20
Henry Emery	35
Marion Griswold	20
Charles Guptil	32
Florence Hannon	25
Irene Jackson	15
Philip Jackson	36
Guy Little	35

Donat Lussier	17
Gordon Miller	32
Virginia Northrup	25
Allen Neil	27
Daniel O'Rourke	20
Roy Robbins	25
Marion Robinson	23
Thomas Rodger	20
Norman Rogers	20
Charles Schaedel	15
John Shea	15
Everett Thiele	15
Mabel (Mae) Weeks	32
Ralph Worcester	25

Starting in 1948, the employees and their spouses gathered at an annual banquet. Clarence has pages of the banquet pictures in his book. With the same people year to year, aging page to page, these photos seem more like a family album. On their Derby's salaries, these clerks and assistant managers bought houses, straightened children's teeth, and sent their children off to college. Half the employees on the list worked at Derby's for twenty-five years or more. The clocks in the marketplace don't keep this kind of time anymore.

IV. Dinosaurs in the Family

The fourth volume shudders to a close like an engine misfiring, snorting and popping out of time before it is still. Sales continue to increase, the store is sold, mismanaged, loses customers, goes into the red, closes.

This fourth volume, "*1970 to The End*," is really the final of the seven binders. (The remaining three volumes on the shelf are appendices to the story: invoices from the 1930s and 1940s, notes on how a small retailer dealt with the New Deal, and "*Over 200 Pictures of Derby's.*") It lacks the verve of the earlier books. In the fourth volume, the sons are running most of the business. Clarence, at age 68, is taking six-week vacations. He, understandably, has less enthusiasm for sales and remodeling. With the retirement of Guy Little, the sales lack the crazy names and the brio he brought to selling. Clarence was also getting older and more tired as he made these books.

Perhaps it is the prominence of his journal notes, but one is more aware of the shoplifting kids and complaining customers. Clarence is on the phone Saturday mornings to remind people to pay their overdue accounts. Almost all do, he says, focusing on the positive, rather than asking, "Why should I have to spend my Saturdays like this?"

Clarence's two sons, John and Charlie, were running the business and they didn't get along. The family decided to sell the store. John sold out his share in 1982 and Charlie a year later. The new owners drained the life out of Derby's, closing departments, losing customers. Derby's went of business in 1985. Clarence took a few pictures of the going-out-of-business sale signs in the front window and he cried. "A nice friendly store that had most everything the ordinary person would want, closed," he said. Clarence made another list: Derby's had survived five wars, the Great Depression, two other depressions, ten recessions, two floods, and a hurricane; Derby's was dead at age 103.

Today there is an art gallery in the Derby's building. Looking at this open and inviting space, it is hard to imagine Clarence and his twenty clerks running a Krazy Days Sale in the narrow aisles of the crowded-shoebox store. The other buildings—the furniture warehouse, the converted railroad freight station that was the scene of the rug sale frenzy, and a beer joint in a transient rooming house—are up-market antique shops and restaurants. Derby's slogan in its early years was "just out of the high-priced district." This is the high-priced district today. The new gallery and stores look great, which is surprising if you know the history of the buildings.

Behind the twinkling white lights and the prim signs, these buildings are just sheds. They were built for storage. Derby's was a shed with a storefront facing the street. The life of commerce moved through the shed. Sheds are malleable. They are undistinguished—they step back and let the contents express themselves. Even the traditional New England meetinghouse is a decorated shed. They were houses, not much more than barns. The worship mattered, not the church. Sheds are vessels of time. We fuss over the architectural details that decorate the store, house, barn, meetinghouse, but we should look more closely at the life that flows through them. The continuous show is inside. *Clarence Derby's USA* defines the life of Derby's in its shed. I wish that we had comparable histories for our other sheds. For each item that lived in the barn, house, meetinghouse, for the harness, cradle, pulpit, and woodstove.

One day a few years ago Charlie Derby came to visit me. He arrived in a 1954 Hudson Hornet, a car puffed out like a marshmallow in the sun, a car swelling with Detroit's Manifest Destiny. The Hudson Hornet seemed determined to stretch from coast to coast even while parked. Charlie had driven his car out to the Midwest and to Canada. In Clarence's book, I had read about the car breaking down in Pennsylvania while Charlie was returning from a hardware show.

The first question I asked him was about a brief entry in the book. When Clarence was in New York City, on one of his many buying trips, in the winter of 1964 there was a snowstorm. Walking in the slippery streets, Clarence had fallen twice. He was out of work for three weeks. That sounded like a severe consequence for falling in the snow.

"He had polio," Charlie said. There's no mention of this anywhere in all those pages, I said. "He didn't talk much about himself," he continued. "He had several operations up to the age of 15, and it's a miracle he was able to walk. It's probably another miracle he was still alive. Amazing he lived to be 92." His bad leg didn't slow him down around the store, where his office was up three flights of stairs. "I'd see him in the basement and he'd say meet me in my office after I talk to Guy. I'd run up the stairs and he'd be there before me. He'd come from the basement, saw Guy, and he got there before me. I never understood how he did it. He'd go up and down those stairs all day. He literally crashed his legs to death trying to walk, because he couldn't walk normally. He didn't walk for the last twelve years of his life." That's when he wrote the loose-leaf binder history. By nature he was a collector; he had a coin collection (and once even ran a Derby's ad looking for a rare 1930 penny). Even though he got around, the polio isolated him. He was active in the Rotary and at church, but since he couldn't golf or ski, he didn't have many close friends, Charlie said. "He was pretty much forced into being a loner a lot of the time."

"What he loved to do is drive. And when the automatic transmission and power brakes and power steering came along, that was right up his alley—because he didn't have to shift. I remember him driving standard shift, having to lift his leg for the clutch—*ugh*—just an effort to do that! And when the automatic came along, he started taking these cross-country trips. He'd go way down to Virginia, to the Civil War battlefields, Revolutionary War battlefields, all up through Canada, Nova Scotia, Cape Breton Island, Quebec. . . . He said he really liked to womp on the gas, just to get that big, throaty V-8 under the hood, stomp it down, feel that *power*! Course in the back, I was a little kid, rocking back and forth—I always got carsick! Always. He bought big cars and he drove them fast! At his funeral my daughter blamed him for lead foot in the family: 'We can trace that back to my grandfather!' We all have it."

Clarence and Charlotte drove across the country many times. They stopped in every state capital. Sometimes they were given a tour of the governor's office and sometimes they met the governor. Clarence would give the governor a Derby's souvenir: a squeeze coin purse, key ring, comb, ashtray, emery board, or a compact sponge. He gave out Derby's souvenirs to people he met all across the country. Clarence would take out his change purse, squeeze out the coins and say, here take this one. Sometimes if they came east, they stopped in to see Derby's.

"It was one of his little tricks," said Charlie. He gave the new charge accounts a little gift box of souvenirs. When someone opened an account at the store and filled out the form, the clerk would tell him or her to go right in and talk with Mr. Derby. "And it didn't take them very long to say, 'You can't do this at Jordan Marsh. You can't go in to talk to Mr. Jordan, you know, or Mr. Macy.' You're talking to the person who owns the store. And they're always impressed—at least most of them were. He used to get quite a kick out of that. He just loved that, people coming in the office. And of course by that time he'd taken all those cross-country trips. He would say, 'Where are you from?' 'Well, I'm from Spokane, Washington—we just moved in.' 'Oh yeah! My car broke down there once! At the Buick garage!' 'Yeah, I know that garage!' Now they've got a friend in Peterborough. Or they'd spent time someplace in Louisiana: 'Yeah—we stayed there one night. Beautiful little town!' I think that's when he was having the most fun, talking to people about where they were from, and things to do and what they're going to do here, all the things we would have in the store. We'd be glad to do anything for them, just come in." Charlie would be sitting in the front office doing the books, listening to his father "gabbing with these new people: Yeah, way to go, Dad, you got another one!

"That's when charge accounts were a little bit different than the way they are now. You could say, charge anything you want, no problem—they'd always pay it. You can't do that now." (Bad accounts were usually half of one percent or less.)

"People's attitudes changed. The people who were here in the thirties, forties, fifties, they were pretty much people you knew. Somebody grew up, graduated from high school, had a job here in town. You dealt with his grandfather, you dealt with his father, you dealt with him, you dealt with his kids." New people moved in, some from the cities, some used to more push-and-shove in their business deals. "Society in general gradually turned to: what can I get out of it for *me*. It's me first. It didn't happen only in Peterborough, it happened around the world. You can't run the type of business he ran the way he ran it." He depended on the loyalty and honesty of his clerks. Customers used to ask for a particular clerk—"Is she in? Well, I'll come back when she's in." And he depended on the honesty of his customers. Stores today have a few closely monitored exits by the cash register. Back then you might pay for your purchase at a register in the middle of the floor and leave by one of many exits. "It didn't occur to anyone to walk out with it."

The world had changed since Clarence's father had advised him to "manage the store easily." "It was good advice at the time it was given, but unfortunately he heeded the advice for too long, because the retail business got extremely complicated. Lechmere, Giant stores, Grants, all the discounters, all the credit cards, telephone shopping, catalogs, and regional malls cropping up. The roads were straighter and smoother and cars were faster. The old hometown was getting a little boring, and so you went to the Mall of New Hampshire and spent most of the day. Attitudes and opportunities changed. It was hard to keep up."

Derby's wasn't changing fast enough, Charlie said. And maybe this time it couldn't change and survive. Derby's was true to its tradition. Clarence believed in having "everything for everybody." "We usually carried a lot of inventory," he said. Charlie had been to college and had worked at Jordan Marsh. He wanted his father to stock less. "I was probably a thorn in his side more than anything else, but I kept pushing him to put in things like inventory control, which is pretty self-explanatory if anybody has half the brain God gave a grapefruit. He just used to go up and down the aisle and say, 'Well, I think I'll order two of those. Maybe a dozen of those.' 'Well how many do you have coming in?' 'I dunno.' 'How many you gonna sell in the next two months?' 'I dunno.' Things like that. You just can't leave the stuff sitting there on the shelf. You gotta get the stuff that moves. Competition was going up.

"I gradually began to see that, oh boy, this is going to be more than I thought. It kind of hit me when I did a survey of department stores like us in northern New England. We went down to Wilson's in Greenfield and sat with them for a couple of hours. Three or four times I did that, got to know them pretty well. When I was in Nashua, I went to Miller's. If this type of business, the family-owned downtown department store, was such a great genre, why weren't more people coming? Finally I found out that the last store of that type to open in New England was Miller's in Nashua in 1929. And I'm thinking, that's the last time somebody opened one of these suckers—not that 1929 was a great time to go into business! But somehow they made it and they survived and I remember the store very well. And I'm thinking, boy, you know, these discounters are growing like weeds. And they were a very good business—I don't like the business—I think it's a horrible way to do business. But man! They're all over the place. By then there was nothing I could do about it. I remember sitting there one night saying, this is a dinosaur. It's going to die on me someday. And it did." After Derby's closed, Charlie managed his own hardware store, and after that a mini-mart. Each business closed. Today he works nights at a gas-and-go mini-mart right next to the town's first shopping center. If you were to turn Derby's upside down, you would have the floodlit nightscape of the always-open mini-mart.

Derby's was an American clock and the clock struck midnight. All the trends we know so well brought down the family store. Most of the time we don't want to go where everyone knows our name. So we're at the mall, in traffic. We choose strangers. Derby's was family. The same clerks for twenty-five years. Go to Peterborough to shop and you could eat in only two places: the diner or Nonie's. Derby's was what you knew; but the rest of the America was booming. Our heart lies with the boom, with the action. Charlie said that he can smell death in a business. We all can. We want to be where it's so busy we complain about the crowds and parking. It's our Coney Island, our Times Square.

We wish that places like Derby's were still there—like the old glass Coke bottle and the Campbell's soup can label—but we reach for the novel, for the same product in a new wrapper. We choose mobility over community. We choose freedom to be unknown. We want anonymous public space. At the mall we are released from time. The mall is a cleaned clock. A mall displaces time with mall time. It distracts you from daylight and exits and keeps you captive, just as casinos do. The stores, one to the next, create a seamless atmosphere of plenty and youth. "At the mall," says consultant Paco Underhill, "we are shopping to stay young."

Charlie misses Derby's. It's where he grew up. He remembers riding his tricycle around the housewares department after hours as his dad did the books. He remembers operating the big old cash register at age nine or ten—*Chunk-chung*—the cash drawer launching out and hitting him in the chest. He remembers the visiting elephant, the pony, Buckets, and the rooster who flew into the river. And he remembers his father telling him that there would always be a Derby's. "I remember thinking at the time, 'Well, I dunno, Dad—nobody ever guarantees that: We'll always be here.'"

In Derby's last years, Clarence saw the competition closing in, but he never gave up his faith that the family business would prevail. They had come through so much—the Depression and the floods—they would adapt. They'd remodel the store, have a sale, continue to make customers into friends.

"All he ever knew was working in the store," said Charlie. "That's all he ever knew. That's all he ever had time to know."

You don't really start in a family business, you awaken to it. It's there in your earliest memories along with the wallpaper in your room and your first toys. And you don't really finish with a family business. You can retire from the business, but not the family. The business is there until you die or the business dies, until one day there are no more Derby's, no more family stores with "everything for everybody." The clock stops. A new clock starts.

Timescape:
Pasture Day

In the early 20th century, cattle kept New Hampshire's mountains open. It was a countryside of panoramic views, groomed like Switzerland. Today it is forest. At the beginning of the summer, cattle were gathered in Concord, Massachusetts, for the three-day walk to pastures just over the border in the New Hampshire towns of New Ipswich and Sharon, and the mountains to the north.

Marion Davis was a cattle drover (and the women's world champion wood chopper in 1936). She lived in New Ipswich with her husband Frank Robbins. "In the spring along the first of May or the last of April we had to begin to mend fences over on the mountain in Sharon and on Barrett Mountain because we were going after cattle the last of the month," Davis told her niece, Connie Hall.

"May 20th was what they used to call Pasture Day—go get the cattle from down country. When we got the fence mending pretty well done, Frank hitched up Sukie. She was a little horse that he had raised from a colt. Grandpa gave her to him and told him he could break her and she was his. So he'd go down to Concord with Sukie and visit the different farmers, find out how many head of cattle they had to come up over the road for pasture through the summer months. A week's notice from then they would meet with their cattle at Meriam's Corner. There was a big barnyard there. We had to get down there the night before because all of those cattle had to be tagged and the descriptions of them set down in a book with their tag number. It took a good long evening job doing it because we generally had around 125 head. Meriam's Corner was in Concord,

Massachusetts, where during the Revolutionary War the men gathered to plan their affairs.

"The next morning we generally left about four o'clock to drive the cattle. We had a man who would go on ahead and take ten or twelve of the cows that had been over the road and knew the route. It was quite a job. Sometimes they'd start ahead and the man that was with them would have to get ahead of them and kind of hold them back a little. It was work keeping them all on the go; it took quite a crew to start us out. We'd wind up at Knops Pond in Groton for the first night's stay. There was a big pasture there that went down to the edge of a pond where the cattle could drink. We'd leave again the next morning and we'd make the Townsend Poor Farm out of West Townsend for the second night. Lots of times when we got there, there'd be another drove of cattle ahead of us that was going up to Stoddard. I remember they had the pasture, and we had to put our cattle in the barnyard, which crowded them some, but we managed all right.

"The next morning we'd make for the mountain. Sometimes we put cattle into the Old Peppermint. That's where there used to be a tavern many years ago. Other times we'd make the top of the hill where the Brown place used to be, where the Wapack Lodge finally wound up. It took us two to three days sorting out the cattle to go to the different pastures. We'd take fifteen to twenty head over to Sharon pasture; there were about 200 acres there. Some went up onto the north end of Barrett Mountain to the Haines pasture, and the rest over to the Reed and Wheeler near the old Livingston place.

"In 1917 we got a Model T Ford. It was one of those that had the brass trim, brass around the lights and on the front of the car. It was the first time we ever used a car to go down country with cattle . . . . It wasn't as much pleasure going down with the car. It wasn't like having old Sukie following along behind."

The last of the cattle drives was around 1920. When the cattle were tagged, they also had to be tested by a veterinarian for TB.

"That was quite a siege because we had to keep them over there for what was called an ear and tail test. They would take blood from the ear and then the tail, and it wasn't a sure test at that. A lot of the cattle reacted to it. I can remember the last little heifer that I had charge of coming up over the road. She lagged, was tired, and I had to push her and keep at her. We got them into the Peppermint. That night it rained and it poured. When we went over, we went in through the gate and there lay the little heifer. . . . She was dead, apparently reacting to the testing.

"But that was years ago. Once they started bringing the cattle up by truck, things were never the same again."

In 1922 Davis and her husband pioneered a hiking trail, the Wapack Trail. Working Sundays between farm chores, they cleared a 21-mile ridge trail. (Davis came up with the name, uniting the starting point at Mount Watatic with the end at North Pack Monadnock.) They later built the Wapack Lodge, which she ran until 1964. She had as many as seventy for a Sunday dinner, and more than a hundred for Thanksgiving and New Year's. Benton MacKaye, the visionary creator of the Appalachian Trail, was an early guest, and he brought students with him to do trail work.

The 91-year-old Davis was honored in 1985 with a trail named for her at the state park on Pack Monadnock. Five generations of her family lined up for a photo that day. She died the next year. The Wapack Lodge, struck by lightning, burned down in 1993. The trail is still a fine walk, thanks to the Friends of the Wapack.

The route that the cattle drovers used to walk in three days is today a busy commuter road. You can drive from the site of Marion Davis' old lodge to Concord, about forty miles, in a little more than an hour.

The Old Homestead

I. Dear Old Joshua

This much is lost: love apples, martin gills, galluses, roundabout suits, separating machines, bootjacks, sasser o'tallers, scarlet runners, Didoes, fannin' mills, and "None o'yer hunker slidin' on me." Those are a few of the words defined in the glossary of the program for the 59th revival of Denman Thompson's *The Old Homestead.* Since 1939, Swanzey, New Hampshire, has performed this play by its hometown hero outdoors in the Potash Bowl. As a few drops of rain fell on my program, I studied the glossary as if it were a menu in a foreign language. There were words for old farming implements, crops, and clothing. A gazetteer of the unknown, the words of one era once so common they were nearly invisible, passing on to a new kind of invisibility.

And this much is known: In 1887 *The Old Homestead* was the hottest ticket in New York. The play ran for more than twenty-five years touring the country, becoming the "greatest popular success of the American stage." From a time before homes were lit by electricity until the time when airplanes were a country-fair attraction, Denman Thompson was playing Uncle Josh Whitcomb to packed theaters. Thompson had added a new character to American folklore. Uncle Josh joined Rip Van Winkle, Davey Crockett, and other outsized 19th-century heroes. Uncle Josh was outsized for his wisdom of staying put. He was the maximum country mouse. "Dear Old Joshua is the very embodiment of honesty and rural simplicity," says his friend in the play.

Thompson made millions of dollars. Uncle Josh appeared in the earliest Edison movies, and his stories were recorded on phonograph cylinders. He advertised Ivory soap. There was even a "Josh Whitcomb" brand cigar. ("As good as the play.")

We sat in a drizzle, rain spitting on and off. There were 82 of us under umbrellas and ponchos huddled on a few rows of wooden benches. When this revival began, thousands filled the natural amphitheater. "Back in the fifties the whole mountain was covered with people. The whole place would be swamped," the play's director for the last 28 years, Jerome Ebbighausen, told me. "I have pictures of it. Just a mass of people. People standing, sitting, the whole hillside was just filled." Upward of 6,000 people would show up for the three nights. Now they hope to draw between 400 and 600. We may be watching a revival and a farewell. In the rain, a visiting town band decamped early, not even staying to play the national anthem.

The play is a catalog of a lost life. True to its name, it is a visit to an old homestead. Thompson packed four acts with the whole rural scene: haying, the old well, milking with a milkmaid singing a milking song, a tramp, a girl from the poor house (Rickety Anne with four giant stage freckles, dressed like Raggedy Anne), a hired hand who is a whistling fool, and two cranky bachelor farmers who spend thirty years courting an old-maid aunt. There are scenes suggesting sleighing in winter and contradancing, and reminiscences of pranks, corny jokes, boyhood wrestling, and the circus coming to a nearby town.

The Old Homestead proceeds like a visit to different exhibits of the nostalgic past. The props are important actors, and the stage is crowded. Moving from stage right to left we see an old oak well bucket, a butter churn, a little white house with green shutters and a green wooden screen door, a rain barrel, a small thumb-back side chair, a Windsor armchair, a painted backdrop of trees and hills, a box representing a well with a bench and dipper in front, a shed with a grinding wheel in front, hay rake, saw, sawbuck, ax in a chopping block, and some cut wood.

There is much talk of chores. We see characters dispatched to milk, call the cows home, bring in wood, and pick berries. Before the curtain rises on Act I, we hear singing from backstage, "Wait for the wagon and we'll all take a ride." We smell the wet oxen (Seth and Josh) as they walk in front of the stage, returning from haying.

The play is also crowded with characters. We are used to seeing three or four actors on stage in two or three acts, often with only one change of scenery. Uncle Josh is supported by fifty characters, major and minor, who are played by twenty actors.

The plot creeps forward like a horse-drawn wagon in thick traffic. The central story is a melodrama about the loss and return of the prodigal son. Uncle Josh's son, Reuben, has left for New York City in shame and has not been heard from. He's become a drunk (Act III). We know that Uncle Josh will go to New York (Act II) and that the son will return (Act IV), but the play keeps a kind of country store time. The action, such as it is, stops for Uncle Josh and the others to reflect on country ways. Remember when the old-timers called tomatoes "love apples"? Remember going barefoot? Remember the cold drink from the old well?

The play also stops several times for the male double quartet to amble in and sing a sentimental favorite. (After a dipper full of water they sing "The Old Oaken Bucket.") In Act I, they enter as the haying crew, each man looking like a Beanie Baby version of a Yankee farmer—gray hair, overalls, plaid or denim shirt, straw hat, red bandana, and a hay fork. Before the show I saw the double quartet leaning against a big wagon backstage, and they looked like what many tourists and journalists still expect to see on their visits. But their faces betrayed them: they were not worn by forty years outdoors. And their overalls were spotless.

In between Acts II and III, Joyce Kilmer's "Trees" was beautifully sung by Joanne Meade in an operatic style (though she had to compete with a police siren). The story around Swanzey is that Kilmer stayed at the Holbrook Farm and was inspired right there to write his famous poem. It's well known that this is not true, but Kilmer did visit the area. "It seems quite possible he could have come to Swanzey," said an elderly man in a bright yellow shirt and a bolo tie who served as the host between acts. "Rumors have some basis in fact; that's how they get started," he said. (Is there a contemporary poem—just one—that any community wants to claim?)

By the time the prodigal son returned home in Act IV, we had been sitting on the hard benches in the rain for two-and-a-half hours. The son is welcomed with a New Year's Eve party. He's reformed himself; he will take over the old homestead. There's an old-time *wow* finish. Uncle Josh comes forward and invites us to visit the old homestead again and "let the scarlet runners chase you back to childhood." They roll up the rug and dance. Moments after the cast took its bows and applauded the audience for staying, the rain let loose in a downpour and we scattered.

"What is the cause of the phenomenal success of this rustic and Christmasy melodrama? What has given it its unprecedented hold upon the affections of the people?" *Current Literature* asked in 1908. Other plays "may come and may go; but *The Old Homestead*, like the immortal brook of Tennyson's poem, goes on forever. . . . The record is unparalleled in the history of the American stage.

"Here is a play that seems to defy every canon of criticism," the magazine's critic said with exasperation. "Its plot, in so far as it may be said to have any plot at all, is as old as the hills. Its technique would be pronounced slovenly by any dramatic expert. It is a melodrama, yet it has no villain and no love-story. The comedy is much of it mere flummery and horse-play."

When the play returned to New York in 1888, more than 290,000 people went to see it in just three months. The reception perplexed the critics. They remarked on the "enormous and vehemently enthusiastic throngs" and noted the play's popularity as you might concede an earthquake under your feet.

Eugene Field, a poet of children's rhymes, knew the secret of the play's power. *The Old Homestead*, he said, is a perfect memory in these "changeful, bitter years:"

Ah! who'd ha' thought the music of that distant childhood time
Would sleep through all the changeful, bitter years
To waken into melodies like Chris'mas bells a-chime!
And to claim the ready tribute of our tears!

Uncle Josh "is an old friend come from among the hills . . . and we seem to breathe once more the atmosphere of those hills, and we seem to hear the humming of bees, and to scent the fragrance of lilacs and wintergreen," Field wrote in his popular *Chicago News* column.

"He does not act—he is," said Field. (Thompson was so natural that when he brought his play back home to New Hampshire, some old Yankees asked for their money back. "It warn't no actin'; it was jest a lot of fellers goin' around and doin' things," they said.)

Thompson's naturalness was praised by William Dean Howells. "The Dean of American letters," a champion of realism, loved the play without reservation. "To be sure, we cannot suppose anyone else playing, or rather being, Joshua Whitcomb with his exquisite perfection. There is not a false note in the old Yankee's personality from first to last; every fiber of the actor's body, as well as every faculty of his mind, seems attuned to its expression; the illusion is without a flaw, and the sense of what is truly fine and good within the rustic simplicity is unbrokenly imparted. It is a surpassingly subtle study," Howells wrote in 1889.

"In fact, on a wider plane than anyone else has yet attempted, Mr. Thompson gives us in this piece a representation of American life." He added, "Of course it is mere suggestion . . . but at its sketchiest it is true, and that is the great matter."

In city after city Howells' praise was echoed. People returned to see the play many times. Some said they couldn't stay away from the theater when the show was in town. One reporter admitted that he had "a perfect mania for the piece." He wrote, "I will confess to dropping into the theater a number of times just to see Joshua and Happy Jack in that seriocomic humorous interview [in Act I]. I never could exactly understand how it happened, but no matter how strong my intention was to stay 'only an act,' I never came away until the strings of Len Holbrook's fiddle had succumbed to asthma in the New Year's night dance in the Old Homestead kitchen. . . . I have been inclined once or twice to find fault with myself for wasting time again and again on a play I have come to know almost by heart . . . I now give myself up completely to the *Old Homestead* habit whenever the show is in town."

Another regular, who knew the dialogue by heart, said, "I now go to watch the people in the auditorium, and never elsewhere have I seen mirth and pathos more distinctly illustrated than in the faces upturned toward Uncle Joshua and his associates."

Uncle Josh Whitcomb brought people home. "The simpler phases of our life still make the strongest appeal to all," wrote Howells. "It is the old homestead in the country which has remained the ideal of a nation tossed in a wilder rush of interests and ambitions than ever tempted men before; the heart yearns forward or backward to it, 'a home of ancient peace,' amidst the turmoil and strife."

People loved seeing the farm. They were delighted by the real oxen. "Dear Uncle Josh Whitcomb," wrote *Pomeroy's Advance Thought* in March 1889. "You are really, now and always, dear old

Uncle Josh. . . . Why don't you have some geese and chickens on that farm, in the first act? And how charming it would be if the handsome Irish assistant could have a real cow to milk in the yard, back of the barn, and in sight of your 4,500 customers. It wouldn't cost you much to add these; and if you had a crow—a live one—to perch on that big tree, and a cat to sit on 'Aunt Matilda's' knee, and a dog, chained and apparently fierce, to take some of the 'bezom' out of that unholy-looking tramp, then the old farm would look more natural and interesting, and we should all want to visit it again and again."

His audience missed geese and chickens and cows and crows.

II. Turn and Jump

The audience wants a familiar novelty. It wants to be surprised by hearing a story it can recognize. It wants the three-cup pea game, the sleight of hand, and look—a pea under each cup! Everyone wins. Dancing dogs, tumbling acrobats, sister acts, comedy, monologues, melodramas, pretty women, and handsome men.

Popular theater "wants to tell us either a truth that we already know or a falsehood we want to believe in," said William Goldman in his candid look at Broadway, *The Season*. The play "must be both fresh and inevitable; you must surprise your audience in an expected way."

Uncle Josh had emerged from thousands of performances—short sketches—during which time Denman Thompson learned to shape the character to please his audience. Or you could say, during this time the audience created Uncle Josh—each night, in different towns, laughing or applauding at what it liked. "You hit upon a bit of business that the audience likes and you retain it," said Thompson. "What they pay no attention, to you leave out or cut short. In that way the play, to a certain extent, molds itself." The variety-show circuit was a theater workshop. Uncle Josh was market-tested.

The variety-show actor worked hard for laughs. He spent days and nights on the train making the "jump" to the next town (or a "broken night jump" if he was required to change trains) for a good "turn" on stage. Turn and jump. Slapstick and knockabout. The language has the feel of rough travel over badly maintained railway track.

There were towns where the actors would "murder 'em" and "leave 'em under their seats." And others where they would "flop," where their act turned to "applesauce," and the audience sat there "handcuffed." There were theaters where they competed with the crashing of bowling pins upstairs, or heavy rain pounding on a tin roof. There were grimy theaters with small, poorly lit dressing rooms so dirty the actors packed a sheet to cover the wall before hanging up their costumes. In the worst places, beer halls and "free and easies," drunken patrons threw food and bottles at the performers. If their act was placed early in the bill, they played to houses preoccupied with settling in, the ushers thunking open seats; placed late they saw only the backs of the audience in retreat. (You need a new finish, one actor was told. A new finish? he replied. No one's ever seen this one.)

The variety actor created his own act and refined it across a thousand nights in a thousand towns. He couldn't turn to a director for advice on the playwright's intentions, and he didn't have three acts to win his audience. In a twenty-minute sketch, a song and dance, a bit of knockabout and slapstick, he had to win them. He was a day laborer, working for the pleasure of the audience.

One turn a night, fifteen or twenty minutes, maybe thirty, then a long wait in stale hotels and gritty railroad cars to think it over: Did they like me? Did they laugh? That bit killed in Buffalo, but died in Cleveland. The players on the variety circuit circled their audience. The audience may have come to see the show, but they were minutely observed by the actors. Stage people were a traveling colloquium on the behavior of crowds. Each discussion sought the same things: to explain the reaction, to please, to wow 'em! Long after the audience in Buffalo or Cleveland had retired to bed and risen to start a new day of work, the actor was still thinking of their reaction to his performance.

The actor on the variety circuit was a ballroom dancer who arrived each night without a partner. Would the audience dance with him, would he wow them? Veteran of a thousand ballrooms, he could never be sure that he wouldn't be a wallflower at his own party, that this would be the night when the dance ended for him. This was Denman Thompson's school.

At age 42 Denman Thompson's career looked as if it were over. He had been on stage for twenty-five years. He had started with the circus as a "property boy," moving the props and with practice appeared as an acrobat. He picked up odd jobs and non-speaking parts before he was hired by a Toronto theater company. The young actor with thick red hair, a round face and "roguish eyes," was "a great favorite" playing Irish comedy, talking with a brogue, and dancing reels and jigs for fourteen years. He also played Uncle Tom in *Uncle Tom's Cabin*, and in blackface, two staples of the stage.

In the middle of a run with *Harry Martin's Varieties* in Pittsburgh, Thompson was bedridden with rheumatism. He could not dance anymore. He was nearly broke, and he had a wife and three children. He had no savings; he always spent what he had and then some. On his wedding day, he didn't even have enough money for the marriage license. That morning he found a job at the Toronto docks shoveling out a cargo of dead hogs. He was late for his own wedding.

Sick, broke, and facing the end of his career, he was comforted by memories of home. He put together a short, two-scene skit. For the lead character, a wise Yankee, he combined the names of two men he had admired back in Swanzey: Joshua Holbrook, a "sturdy, sedate farmer," and Captain Otis Whitcomb, celebrated for his wit at town meeting. (In the program for the Swanzey revival, Arthur Whitcomb advertises "blocks-pavers-bricks.")

The owner of *Harry Martin's Varieties* took pity on the aging comedian. He let him perform as Uncle Josh in a benefit show to raise money for himself. (Benefits were a theater tradition.) Thompson hobbled on stage using a cane. Uncle Josh was a hit; he was held over for two weeks, "It took like wildfire," said Thompson.

Uncle Josh had begun his travels. Thompson added a few characters in Rochester, New York. In Chicago in 1876 and 1877, he added two acts. *Joshua Whitcomb*, now bulked up to three acts, and running 2 hours 10 minutes, flopped. He toured the play in New England. It flopped again. Thompson kept rewriting the play, adjusting his performance like the variety-show trouper that he was.

In *Joshua Whitcomb*, Uncle Josh delivers a wagonload of pumpkins in Boston. He meets Tot, a poor street-sweeper girl whose drunken stepfather beats her. Uncle Josh promises her dying mother that he will rescue Tot. He also dispatches the villain as he attacks once more, tossing him through a window. Tot comes back to Swanzey with the old farmer and marries his son.

Thompson was working familiar territory. The stage Yankee was born along with theater in America. The first comedy written by an American, *The Contrast* by Royall Tyler in 1787, featured the Yankee Jonathan, who would beget many Jonathans, practical and patriotic, ready to sing *Yankee Doodle* and to puncture the pretensions of the obliging British snob. The 19th century saw a parade of rubes on stage: Solomon Swap, Solon Shingle, Nathan Yank, Adam Trueman, Deuteronomy Dutiful, Industrious Doolittle, Jedediah Homebred, Horsebean Hemlock, Hiram Dodge, Obediah Whitcher, Obadiah Squash, Asa Trenchard, Eli Wheatfield, Old Jed Prouty, and Lot Sap Sago, as well as a flock of Jonathans (Jonathan Ploughboy, Jonathan Postfree, etc.), and after Thompson, a flock of "Uncle" shows.

By Thompson's time, the stories were usually the same. A rube (many times that's his name, Reuben—Rube for short) comes to the big city where much confusion and hilarity ensue—sometimes with song-and-dance numbers in tenement roof gardens. The rube, even though confused by ordinary city habits, teaches the city slickers a thing or two and returns home.

Thompson took his play out west. In Denver in 1878 they began to warm up to Uncle Josh. His first night he played to a half-empty theater. By the third night it was full. He stayed for eight weeks. Thompson pushed on to the Pacific and in San Francisco he was a hit. Uncle Josh had finally connected with his audience. He returned east and was a hit in New York.

Thompson had put away the Irish brogue and the blackface. He had learned from an old actor that the "highest art is to conceal art." He had watched as that old actor walked and talked on stage just as people do in life. The performance haunted him. In the first skit, Uncle Josh had dressed in a clownish, exaggerated manner. He refined his act. Uncle Josh copied his "grandfather's clothes to a crease": baggy pants, a shirt with an open vest, a straw hat, and boots (which he wore on stage for thirty-five years). He wore no stage make-up. Denman Thompson had gone to school for years and Uncle Josh was his valedictory address.

Joshua Whitcomb toured for eight years. The public wanted more. Other rural plays foundered; other stage Yankees were spurned. The public welcomed Uncle Josh as authentic. Thompson wrote *The Old Homestead* with George Ryer, adding more characters drawn from his Swanzey days. Thompson was overflowing with stories, said Ryer, "one-half of which, if I could remember, would adorn and prosper several plays."

By the time *The Old Homestead* debuted in Boston and New York, many people knew Uncle Josh. He was a familiar character in a new setting. They loved Uncle Josh and they forgave *The Old Homestead* its many faults. "I think the title was a fortune in itself," said Ryer.

Thompson prospered. (Ryer had sold out early for $2,500.) He paid his old debts from his wilder Toronto days, advertising to alert his creditors. Uncle Josh became part of the culture, honored with songs like *Uncle Josh's Huskin Dance* and burlesqued by Dockstader's Minstrels in *The Old Bedstead*. He appeared in advertisements like this one in which Uncle Josh is at the theater. He asks his neighbor why Lady Macbeth is wringing her hands:

"It's Duncan's blood," the man replied,
"She strives the fearful stains to hide."
"Why don't she wash her hands, b'gosh!
With Ivory Soap?" cried Uncle Josh.

III. The Changeful, Bitter Years

In Act II, when Uncle Josh goes to the city to find his son, he stays with his boyhood friend Henry Hopkins, who has become a millionaire. We see Hopkins' fancy parlor with a marble statue, bearskin rug, plush chairs, and a servant who is summoned with a bell. ("Why don't you hang the bell around his neck, that way you'll know where he is," Uncle Josh says.)

He and Henry get to talking over the old days. There is an urgency in reminiscence; the pace quickens in recollection:

Josh: Do you remember the first circus you and I ever went to see?

(Both laugh heartily—Josh falls back on the divan—then recovers himself; rubs top of his head with both hands and then sinks back laughing as though he was exhausted from laughing.)

Henry: (laughing) And how we laughed at the old clown!

Josh: And et ginger bread!

Henry: Yes.

Josh: Henry, do you remember that?

Henry: Remember it? I shall never forget it as long as I can remember anything.

Josh: Me nuther! I spent forty-one cents that day!

Henry: We went together, don't you remember?

Josh: So we did!

Henry: I called for you at your house.

Josh: There! That's right.

Henry: It was the first you ever wore a roundabout suit.

Josh: (proudly) So it was!

Henry: Oh, you were dressed to kill that day!

Josh: Gosh! I guess I was! You had on a new store hat and I had to wear the old one [Aunt Matilda] braided. You beat me on the hat but I kind o' cut you on the clothes. (Chucks Henry in ribs—both laugh.)

Henry: Yes.

Josh: Both of us barefoot.

Henry: Yes, both of us.

(Josh gives Henry affectionate shove.)

Henry: And away we both started for Keene and the circus (with pathos) and don't you remember, Joshua, that when we got on top of that little hill, near Jackson's, we looked back and there was your dear old mother, standing in the doorway. (Rising and folding his hands in pantomime.) Her hands wound up in her apron, with her head thrown back, the way she had a way of doing, looking at us through her big, bowed spectacles, wondering, I suppose, which one of us would be president first. (Sitting down.)

Josh: (With feeling, shaking hands with Henry and looking over glasses) Happy days, Henry!

Henry: Happy, indeed, Joshua.

His audience had made that trip, too. They had walked away from their homes. They had left their village by foot, by horse, by canal boat, and rail. And here they were in a harsh new land, immigrants from the farm among immigrants from Europe. Just as the European immigrants maintained their old-country ties, so did these immigrants, meeting in groups like the New England Society of Brooklyn, and the Sons of New Hampshire. They sang *Home, Sweet Home,* and *The Old Oaken Bucket.* They knew *Woodman, Spare That Tree!,* and they listened to Oliver Wendell Holmes' reminiscences about his country childhood, making him one of the better-paid lecturers on the lyceum circuit. "O', the remembrance of the early days passed amidst these holy scenes!—of tumbling in long grass, and sucking of honeyed clover, and burrowing in mountainous haycocks and climbing elbowed trees; of waking to the clamor of twittering swallows, and sleeping at the curfew of purring crickets," Holmes declaimed. "Let him tread the grass for fifteen summers, and then plod the pavement for forty years, and his dream will still be of running barefoot among the clover." Regret is the literature of progress.

The reunion of the millionaire and the farmer "is one of the most beautifully veracious we remember on stage," wrote William Dean Howells. "We could not praise it too much; in conception and execution it is a masterpiece . . . we should confidently trust it to move any man who had kept his boyhood uncontaminate in his heart."

His audience had made that trip, but they could not reunite the millionaire and the farmer. The politics of the era could not achieve that reunion either.

The Old Homestead was a time play, it was a clock. Its slow pace was the real story: Look at how slowly time used to pass. We had time to chat. We were barefoot. We did chores. On the stage Uncle Josh is a man who owns his time. He does not answer to a clock, to an overseer or foreman. Out in the street, there were time battles, time wars, fights for work and wages.

Denman Thompson had written his first play, *Joshua Whitcomb,* in hard times. The Panic of 1873 led to the longest depression in the country's history. By 1877 there were approximately five million people unemployed. Only one-fifth of the labor force had regular employment.

Wages were cut by as much as forty-five percent. There were hard-fought strikes in textiles, coal mining, cigar making, and the railroads.

The railroads had cut wages a second time that decade, setting off the first national strike in 1877. The Great Strike spread quickly. Mills and furnaces were forced to close. There was fighting in the streets of Baltimore and Pittsburgh, slaughter in Chicago and Reading, a riot and the surrender of the militia in Harrisburg, arson in Philadelphia and Cincinnati, attacks on the militia in Buffalo, and threats to federal troops in Jersey City. More than one hundred were killed. Nine state governors called the railroad strike an insurrection and sent for federal troops to keep the trains running. The governors couldn't rely on their state militias. Some 45,000 militia in eleven states were called out, but some had stacked arms, refusing to march against citizens. The rich felt as if they were living atop a land mine. "Any hour the mob chooses it can destroy any city in the country—that is the simple truth," John Hay wrote to his father-in-law. Hay later served as assistant secretary of state.

"We are in the earlier stages of a war upon property, and upon everything that satisfies what are called the higher wants of civilized life," Unitarian minister Jonathan Baxter Harrison wrote in 1878, calling attention to "Certain Dangerous Tendencies in American Life." The chief danger, he said, was not rioting, but mob rule destroying representative government.

In the press and in private, there was talk of limiting suffrage. "All honest, thoughtful men know that the ballot must be restricted, and I suppose that can be done only through blood," the U.S. District Judge for Indiana wrote in a letter. "Democracy is now the enemy of law & order & society itself & as such should be denounced." The founding fathers had gone "too far with their notions of popular government," said the judge.

The Great Strike had shown the fierce divisions in the country. The president of the nation's most powerful company, the Pennsylvania

Railroad, proposed permanently garrisoning troops in cities "at prominent points" and building armories. After the strike, the state militias were re-created as the National Guard. The War Department published a booklet on "riot duty." (A private pamphlet was circulating: "Suggestions Upon the Strategy of Street Fighting.") Armories were built in major cities. In Chicago, businessmen raised money and levied a tax to build and support an armory.

The treasurer of the Gatling Gun Company wrote to the president of the Baltimore and Ohio Railroad, which had been besieged during the strike: "One Gatling, with a full supply of ammunition, can clear a street or track, and keep it clear." The railroad's reply is not recorded, but there were sales elsewhere. Pennsylvania's governor ordered the machine guns for his reorganized National Guard. *The Independent*, a journal of the Congregational Church, concurred. "If the club of the policeman, knocking out the brains of the rioter, will answer, then well and good; but if it does not promptly meet the exigency, then bullets and bayonets, canister and grape . . . constitute the one remedy and one duty of the hour. . . . Napoleon was right when he said the way to deal with a mob is to exterminate it."

One month after *The Old Homestead*'s April 1886 debut in Boston, a bomb exploded in Chicago's Haymarket Square as the police were dispersing a small, quiet labor rally. The bomb knocked down rows of policemen; windows were shattered for blocks around. The police rose and fired wildly into the crowd for several minutes, killing seven or eight civilians, wounding thirty to forty (no one is sure). Sixty police were injured, and seven died. Most of the injuries, and at least three of the dead police, were from police gunfire.

Chicago panicked. The city was gripped with "one of the strangest frenzies of fear that ever distracted a whole community," recalled one witness. Three hundred leading citizens pledged $100,000 to eliminate anarchists and supported the fund for the next five years.

The police raided the homes and meeting places of suspected radicals without search warrants. They beat and tortured suspects and jailed them for days without charges. "Make the raids first and look up the law afterward!" advised the state's attorney, Julius S. Grinnell. For eight weeks Chicago was under martial law. Editors of anarchist newspapers were arrested, mail was opened and read, trade union meetings were banned, public gatherings were outlawed. The color red was forbidden in any advertisements.

In the national hysteria that followed, the press called for revenge. "In the early stages of an acute outbreak of anarchy a Gatling gun, or if the case be severe, two, is the sovereign remedy," suggested *The New York Times*. The anarchists were guilty: A double-page drawing in *Harper's Weekly* showed the workers firing into the police.

The year had begun with strikes and riots in the coal fields of southwestern Pennsylvania, followed by strikes at Chicago's McCormick Reaper Works and by New York's streetcar workers. The police drove the streetcars through the barricades. In railroad yards in Texas and East St. Louis, a railroad strike led to rioting. In Milwaukee, the militia guarding a mill fired into labor marchers, killing five, wounding a dozen. By the end of 1886 there had been 1,400 strikes involving a half million workers. Forty-five percent of industrial workers were barely above the poverty line. "The workers are on the eve of an uprising," Edward Bellamy warned in a postscript to his Utopian novel *Looking Backward*, published that year. There were close to 37,000 strikes on record from 1881 to 1905.

These strikes were time wars, say some labor historians. We tend to think of strikes for wages and benefits, but "some of the most dramatic and significant events in the history of labor, such as the strikes of 1886, the Haymarket riots . . . were part of this century-long struggle for shorter hours," wrote Benjamin Kline Hunnicutt in *Work Without End*. Workers resented losing control of their time—how long they worked and how that work was done. On the farm they had worked until the chore was completed or they went hunting or fishing. Work was measured by the task, not by the hour. They resisted the new industrial order with "absenteeism, irregular work habits, and celebration of a long list of traditional holidays and special occasions, all of which plagued industrial managers," wrote Hunnicutt. The English historian E. P. Thompson called this resistance, "the struggle against time."

This struggle was so serious that in 1886, the architect of total war, General William Tecumseh Sherman, predicted, "There will soon come an armed contest between Capital and Labor. They will oppose each other not with words and arguments and ballots, but with shot and shell, gunpowder and cannon. The better classes are tired of the insane howlings of the lower strata and they mean to stop them."

"The eighties dripped with blood," wrote the reformer Ida Tarbell, "and men struggled to get at causes, to find corrections, to humanize and socialize the country; for then as now there were those who dreamed of a good world although at times it seemed to them to be going mad."

Eight anarchists were arrested for the Haymarket bombing. The jury found them guilty and sentenced seven to die, even though there was no evidence. (The bomb thrower was never caught.) Four were hanged, one committed suicide. The remaining three were pardoned six years later. "Annie," Howells wrote to his sister, "it's all been an atrocious piece of frenzy and cruelty for which we must stand forever ashamed before history...."

Anxious times. A pioneering neurologist said Americans were uniquely nervous. "American nervousness is the product of American civilization. The Greeks were certainly civilized, but they were not nervous, and in the Greek language there is no word for that term," wrote Dr. George Beard in *American Nervousness, Its Causes and Consequences* (1881). His book, and his newspaper articles, found a willing readership. Beard's theory was contradictory, as commodious as a popular play or song—one could see what one wanted to—and it was widely adopted.

The telegraph, the railroad, and the rush of information pushed Americans in a new hurried pace, commentators said. (Thompson promoted a small cigar, "Between Acts"—"Particularly satisfying . . . when time is limited.") The noisy city "kept the nerves jangling day after day and night after night" and cut people off from what they saw as the real life of the farm and country—"Newyorkitis," Dr. John H. Girdner called it in 1901. Businessmen worked themselves to nervous collapse or suicide, said the philosopher Herbert Spencer, who had suffered nervous exhaustion for years. "Everywhere I have been struck with the number of faces which told in strong lines of the burdens that had to be borne," Spencer said in 1882. "Something must be done—this is universally admitted—to lessen the strain in modern life," said *Harper's Monthly* in 1894.

The Old Homestead was one cure. It had the "healing properties of precious memories," wrote James Jay Brady in a souvenir biography of Thompson. "The tired eye, dull skin, nervous manner, unsettled feelings . . . are banished."

In 1892 the word *Homestead* had a new meaning. At Andrew Carnegie's steel mill in Homestead, Pennsylvania, when the union protested a wage cut, they were locked out. The plant manager, Henry Clay Frick, sent in a private army of three hundred Pinkerton guards. At the end of a daylong battle, nine strikers and seven guards were dead. The Pinkertons surrendered and were beaten by the crowd. But Frick prevailed; the nation's largest trade union was defeated. This domestic warfare shocked the country and Congress launched two investigations.

This was the world outside Uncle Josh's barnyard. The play grew in popularity through the 1890s. *The Old Homestead* was welcomed wherever it toured. In September 1890, it returned for its fourth long season in New York. A year later it began a twelve-week run at the Boston Theatre. The railroads ran special excursion trains from six states. Country people, who never went to the theater, saved up to go see "the play of the century." In the final week "there was not a single "'deadhead'" (unpaid seat) in the house," said the theater manager. "No theater in the world had ever before played to so much money in one week at the prices, which ranged from twenty-five cents to one dollar and a half." December 1891 to January 1892: three weeks in Brooklyn. "An astonishing run for Brooklyn." September 1892: Boston, eight weeks, "large receipts." January 1893: Philadelphia, seven weeks. "The most remarkable dramatic record ever made in this city." September 1894: Boston, seven weeks, "another phenomenal engagement . . . very large returns." September 1896: Boston, seven weeks, "customary large business." And on into the first years of the new century, playing to packed theaters in Pittsburgh, Chicago, San Francisco, and elsewhere. Demand was strong; Thompson cast a second company to tour the smaller cities. The manager of both the Boston Theatre and the Academy of Music in New York added it up: 1,345 performances at just those two theaters, with receipts totaling $1.39 million.

IV. Where Is My Wandering Boy Tonight?

The principal action in *The Old Homestead* is sitting. Or as Uncle Josh pronounces it, sawt down. Pull up a chair, let's talk. Of all the barnyard details and the oxen, the chair is the key prop. Here is my count, by those doing the inviting: Aunt Matilda, one; Henry Hopkins, one (to Josh); and Uncle Josh, five, which includes an invitation to two characters. "Git a chair and set down," he says. It's one of his most frequent lines. *The Old Homestead* is a sermon against restlessness. Its a paean to hearth and home, and to simple country folks. He played the kind of wise man he had once known, the kind audiences wanted to believe was out there in the villages.

His audiences wanted to sit awhile. Of course Denman Thompson would have to tour the country for years talking about setting. He made his living portraying the kind of settled life he had briefly known. His past, like his audience's, was unsettled.

The Thompson family homestead was more like a pitched tent than the abiding calm center audiences saw. His parents were restless. Denman's great-great-grandfather was one of the earliest settlers in Swanzey. Three generations of Thompsons were living in town when Denman's newly married parents, Rufus and Ann, headed west in 1831. They settled in a small hamlet on the Pennsylvania frontier near Lake Erie, cleared the land, and built a log cabin. Two years later their first son, Henry Denman, was born. Two sisters and one brother followed. They were always poor. The family returned to Swanzey in defeat when Denman was fourteen. He received his formal schooling—three winter terms—did farm chores, pulled pranks, saw the circus, and, when he was seventeen, he left for Boston. He had lived in Swanzey just three years, but out of that he fashioned his life's work, the character of Uncle Josh.

When he returned to New Hampshire with the play many years later to a triumphant homecoming, his parents had long since left the Swanzey homestead to try their luck out west again. Thompson toured the house, deeply moved, a lump in his throat, said those with him.

The Old Homestead may be a dream-play—the daydream of an actor on the road, dreaming of a settled life he could never have.

Sitting awhile in the barnyard was especially appealing during the years of upheaval after the Civil War. Home was a dream. Men roamed the countryside looking for work during the long depression of the 1870s. One scholar estimates that between ten and twenty percent of the population were from families in which one member had tramped for work. By the winter of 1875 private soup kitchens in large cities were overwhelmed. "What an ocean of misery," said *The National Labor Tribune* in America's centennial year.

Tramps were feared. "The tramp menace" was "the curse of our Yankee nation." Tramps were a "dangerous class . . . at war with all social institutions," said professor Francis Wayland of Yale, who blamed the Great Strike of 1877 on the "great standing army of professional tramps." At a conference in Saratoga Springs in 1877, the heads of charitable organizations, academics, and businessmen responded to the crisis. They agreed to cut relief, aiming to eliminate the "undeserving poor."

Many other solutions were offered: Shoot them, poison them, flood them. "The best meal that can be given to the regular tramp is a leaden one," suggested one writer in *The New York Herald*. "A little strychnine or arsenic in the meat and other supplies furnished the tramp," advised *The Chicago Tribune*. Murder them and let their bodies fertilize your fields, suggested *The Minneapolis Tribune*. Or let the tramp work for his own salvation. A popular writer suggested placing the man in a cistern flooding with water and making him pump himself out. "If he worked he was saved, and if he refused he was drowned." Connecticut posted a five-dollar bounty on tramps. Ohio sentenced tramps to three years in jail for trespassing or starting a fire on the highway. The Ohio Supreme Court upheld the law, saying "the genus tramp, in this country, is a public enemy. He is numerous and dangerous. . . . He is a thief, a robber, often a murderer, and always a nuisance. . . ." Other states passed new laws to fight the "tramp evil." *The Railroad Gazette* applauded all efforts to "exterminate these pests."

Uncle Josh had a different reaction. In Act I, a tramp appears in the barnyard. At the mention of a tramp in the area, a visiting girl screams "Tramps? Why, we'll all be robbed" and races into the house. Uncle Josh meets the tramp. He is cautious at first.

Josh: Who be you?

Jack: (bows low) A man without a home; poor, but a gentleman still.

Josh: You're a tramp I guess, ain't you?

Jack: Well, vulgarly speaking, yes, properly, no!

Josh: What be you?

Jack: A natural result.

Josh: Of what?

Jack: Drink!

Uncle Josh admires his honesty. He invites Happy Jack to pull up a chair and set. He gives the tramp two slices of bread and butter. Happy Jack tells Josh how his friend was killed riding between the wheels (on the truck) under the railroad car. "I was riding on the rear truck and he on the front. In rounding a curve the brace of the truck bent and . . . mashed him to death. I had to ride nearly thirty miles listening to his pitiful cries for help, but I couldn't reach him."

Happy Jack reminds Uncle Josh of his lost son. He asks the tramp about his family. Happy Jack says he cannot go home because he is ashamed. "I'm no good. A wreck at twenty-five; look forty, don't I?" Uncle Josh offers him money if he'll buy his fare home and give up drinking: "All right—sir, there's a five dollar bill. It won't break me and it may make you."

The curtain comes down on Uncle Josh lamenting his lost son. Offstage we hear a hymn, *Where Is My Wandering Boy Tonight?* which the show made popular (as it also did with *Rock-A-Bye-Baby*). In earlier productions, the double quartet sang the hymn while a "dreamlike vision" appeared center stage of the lost son drinking at a bar.

Oh, where is my wand'ring boy tonight,
The joy of his mother's pride?
He's treading the ties with his bed on his back,
Or else he's bumming a ride. . . .
He's on the head-end of an overland train,
That's where your boy is tonight.

The Old Homestead was a place where the pulpit met the stage, said one review. Thompson said that "thousands" had told him they had been "moved to a new sense of moral obligations." In an era when the theater was suspect, only plays with a moral were acceptable for proper folks. Many of the long runs had messages: *Uncle Tom's Cabin,* slavery is evil. *Ten Nights in a Barroom* and *The Drunkard*, drinking is evil.

A souvenir biography of Thompson carried "good words from the clergy." "I have seen it twice, and have advised my people, more particularly the young men's guild and the older boys of the Sunday school to go and see it," said the Rev. Edward Wallace Neil, Church of St. Andrew-the-Martyr. "I consider your play equal to a dozen sermons. . . . "

The Old Homestead turns out to be also a temperance tract. "Drink is the ruination of more than half the young men of New York," we are told. Two male characters are rescued from drink, and quite easily it seems, with a little advice from Uncle Josh, a spot of cash, and some pluck. Happy Jack the tramp makes the transition from torn rags to top-hatted swell in just three weeks! (He does tell us that he has a wealthy mother, thus evading the sticky matter of working.) And Josh's son, Reuben, is turned around by his father's visit. Temperance it appears is simply a matter of resolve. When offered a hand, people pick themselves up, dust themselves off, and start all over again.

"It is an unadorned fact that a number of young men have been reclaimed from the habit of drink by the powerful effect of situations and scenes in this play," claimed the souvenir biography.

The reporter who confessed to having "a perfect mania" for the show, also wrote: "A pious man is said to regard Lent as a season during which he shall try to be a little better than his nature. I am not ashamed to say that I approach this 'eight weeks run' in a somewhat similar spirit. It is a time when a young man may stand in front of himself and scrutinize his own being. Are his habits of life correct? Are his sympathies deep enough? Is his conception of human existence a full one? And for the father, as for the son, there are suggestions for honest self-questioning."

Uncle Josh reassured audiences. They had grown up well and could return to that Eden. Tramps and drunks were someone's child, someone's spouse. Simple Josh presides over homecomings: farmer and millionaire, tramp and society, father and son. With his last lines, he steps toward the lip of the stage and addresses the audience: "Now, you fathers that have got wild boys, I want you to be kind o' easy with them. If they are kind o' foolish now and then, forgive them. Like as not, it is as much your fault as 'tis theirs—they might have inherited it, you can't tell."

In an era of orations that lasted two hours, a time when words were fire and war, Uncle Josh was the anti-orator. Foreigners remarked on the rough trade of American speech. "Democracy everywhere has no soft words . . . it confuses moderation with weakness, violence with heroism," Frenchman Michael Chevalier said fifty years before Uncle Josh's day. "Never was oratory more orotund, propaganda more reckless, denunciation more bitter, reform more strident," said historian Howard Mumford Jones. While politicians and preachers roamed the pulpit, Josh set down and listened. He was neighborly. He was avuncular. In an increasingly aggressive culture, Uncle Josh was kind.

V. The Dearest Place on Earth

Denman Thompson lived in a very large house. He dwelled in his success. Reporters came to visit and in long portraits marveled over the house and its extensive grounds. Naturally, you would want to know about the home of the man who was *The Old Homestead*. He is just like Uncle Josh, they said. In the summer he liked to sit in the shade of the barn with his chair tilted back against the wall and chat with neighbors. "In growing old, Denman Thompson has acquired what might be called the look of goodness," wrote William Walsh of his visit with the 77-year-old Thompson the year before he died. He had begun building his house in 1879, a year after his first success with *Joshua Whitcomb*. He bought the homestead where his mother was born. “This is, of course, the dearest place on earth to me,” he said. His house was built around the old farmhouse, just as his success was built around the memory of that homestead. The old house had a large kitchen that was the model for the country kitchen in Act IV.

Thompson’s home was not confined to the small comforts of farm life. It was a Victorian home, an exaggeration of comfort; the house with its awnings out like sails, big porches, big rooms crowded with furniture. The outside world of factory and city had grown larger, and the house matched it.

His house was lavish: gilded furniture in the front parlor, a black marble fireplace in Thompson’s office, a marble statue in the broad front hallway, a library, a big recreation room with two pool tables, a greenhouse for flowers, stables, a hay barn, a large outdoor doll-house, and, down by the Ashuelot River, a tower to observe the countryside. The “far-rolling lawns” and gardens were fronted by a stone wall and 400 feet of cement road, said to be the first paved road in New Hampshire, and paid for by Thompson. He paid for many other improvements around town.

“Yes, it’s all very fine,” he told a *Los Angeles Times* reporter, “but we live in the barn.” The family had set up a living room in the front section of the stable for hot summer weather. A birdcage with a canary hung on each side of the barn door. By the Fourth of July they moved to a colony of cottages by the lake. An old farmhouse served his extended family as a dining pavilion. In another building there were two bowling alleys. His children and their spouses, who acted in the show and managed the business, all lived nearby, as did his father. He owned seven houses all in a row for relatives.

For years he continued to add to the house and the grounds. Six or seven men were usually working on the place. When Thompson was home, he liked to work with the men. He also kept a farm, where the two oxen that toured with the company summered. He loved animals. Each morning the horses whinnied for their lump of sugar, and an orphan lamb cried at the back door for a bottle. A reporter pointed out a pet rabbit in the garden eating a cabbage. "Oh, never mind," Thompson answered. "We will never miss one, and he probably wants it or he wouldn't take the trouble to eat it."

Uncle Josh at home made for a pleasing portrait, but he really lived on the road. The railroad made Thompson's touring company possible. The railroad had created Uncle Josh, and his audience. He spent so much time on trains that he even patented a device to prevent railroad accidents. (Spare wheels that would have required two extra rails.)

The poor boy had made good, and made it the hard way. By his own estimate, he had played Uncle Josh in the skits and plays an average of ten times a week, forty weeks a year, for thirty-five years. He had played Uncle Josh 15,000 times and didn't stop until he had to leave the stage after a heart attack in Boston in 1911.

If his accounting is correct, Thompson is the Iron Man of the American theater. Joseph Jefferson played *Rip Van Winkle* 5,000 times and was beloved. He fished with the president and was mourned on his passing. Eugene O'Neill's father, James, played *The Count of Monte Cristo* in 6,000 performances and was ruined. "We almost died doing it," said a member of his cast.

We might think it was a prison of repetition. Fifteen thousand days and nights in the same barnyard with long-suffering Aunt Matilda, grumpy Cy Prime, Happy Jack, Reuben the prodigal son, Rickety Anne, Whistling Eb, and the others.

But Thompson put off retirement. "I have set the limit at 94 and perhaps by that time I will set the limit at a hundred," he said when he was 77. In his scrapbook of morals, there is this entry: "The best antidote against melancholy is occupation." Like many once-poor actors, he couldn't stop working. He wrote other plays with George Ryer, but not one was adopted by the audience. He was Uncle Josh, the "embodiment of a national tradition." On stage Uncle Josh invited the audience to sit with him. That was his showmanship. He had come from the farm, not the hotel and the railroad station. That's the fairy tale.

Timescape:
False Witness

In the center of a small New England city is a timescape of war. At the head of Main Street in Keene, New Hampshire, just opposite the common, is a flagpole on a traffic island. It is an expected sight, so it sits largely unseen. The flagpole rises from a polished red granite base with a bronze plaque that declares:

Keene Remembers

The Colonial Wars
1675–1763

Revolutionary War
1775–1783

War with England
1812–1814

War with Mexico
1846–1848

Civil War
1861–1865

War with Spain
1898–1902

Mexican Expedition
1916–1918

World War
1917–1918

And Its Citizens
Who Served

This monument is a solemn promise and a lie. Do Keene's citizens rise each morning, look into the mirror, and remember the dead of eight wars? No. No one can. On Memorial Day or Veterans' Day, do they remember all the way back to 1675? No.

The first remembrance is already a forgetting. Hiding behind "The Colonial Wars" are King Philip's War, Bacon's Rebellion, King William's War, Queen Anne's War, Tuscarora War, Yamasee War, King George's War, French and Indian War, and Pontiac's War. Hiding behind this one generic listing is the history we don't want to remember.

Four Centuries of King Philip's War

I. One Sunday Afternoon

Turners Falls comes at you with an eerie familiarity, an American place déjà vu. Crossing the narrow bridge over the Connecticut River, the town is laid out with the promise of a prosperous small republic. It's a triumphal entrance. There's the wide main street ahead, a skyline of church spires, and a rising green hill with a row of commanding Victorian houses. Below, off to the left, is a park along the river, a generous green space. The river is wide here, more like a harbor, glinting with reflected sunlight. To the right, below the dam, is an old redbrick mill. Everything about the place resonates with a seen-before, handled-before quality. We know this place deep in our American hearts.

I have come to this Massachusetts mill town without expectation, without knowing anything about it. I am on my way home, taking a detour to find a used bookstore. The town stops my journey, detours my detour. It feels like something terrible has happened here. I sense so many notes of anguish.

On this Sunday late in May, nothing on the main street, Avenue A, is open except one or two stores selling used goods, rummage sale rejects. One store advertises in faded letters: You Deserve The Best. A man and a child are sitting out front, time heavy on their hands. You know they are poor and cannot join in the parade of mobility that rushes through the town, cars loaded with bicycles, kayaks, and canoes.

On the streets behind Avenue A are three-story apartment buildings and houses kneeling behind crumbling porches. Many houses show long tenure and care; others disorder and neglect. The big houses, once home to the mill bosses, doctors, and lawyers, are up on the heights. Turners Falls was once a bigger place.

I drive around the town four times—down by the old mill and railroad tracks, up by the heights—drive as if in a dream. Turners Falls spooks me. I have no idea why. I wait at a traffic light with only two flashy motorcycles beside me. The street is empty. The light seems to be red forever. It's Sunday afternoon, 3 p.m. I have to leave. I can't stand to be in Turners Falls any longer. Minutes ago my eyes scanned the main street, alert for architectural ornament, for the rhythm of the street; now I feel as if I have been here forever.

Many years later I learned that four hundred people were murdered here.

On May 19, 1676, hundreds of Indians were encamped at the falls to fish for salmon heading up river. It was an ancient meeting: Indians and salmon had been coming here for thousands of years.

On that morning Captain William Turner and 150 men surprised the sleeping Indians. They fired into wigwams and chased fleeing old men, women, and children into the river and the falls where they drowned or were shot. Turner and his men burned the camp, destroyed stored food, two small forges for repairing guns, and lead to make shot. They took no prisoners.

On their retreat, a couple of miles from the falls, Turner and thirty-eight of his men were killed. He was an outcast, a tailor by trade, who had been denied a commission at first. He had been jailed twice for his Baptist beliefs. One day's bloody work is his only contribution to history. The English celebrated the slaughter as a great victory in King Philip's War.

For years I have traveled through the landscape of war, unawares. Applying the words "King Philip's War" to a map of New England is like the childhood game of writing with magic ink to reveal a secret message. Words that we associate with distant wars appear in the ordinary places we live or visit: attack, murder, massacre.

King Philip's War was a short, ferocious war. The Wampanoag sachem Metacom, or King Philip, led an uprising against the English colonies in Massachusetts, Rhode Island, parts of Connecticut, and Maine. Metacom's father, Massasoit, had been a great friend and ally to the Pilgrims at Plymouth. He had given them seed corn and taught them about gathering food. The Pilgrims would have starved without Massasoit. He is the Indian chief portrayed at the "first thanksgiving." Fifty years of peace followed Massasoit's treaty with the Pilgrims in 1621, but by Philip's time, the English population was growing faster than almost any other in the world, and they were pushing for more land.

"The English who came first to this country were but a handful of people, forlorn, poor, and distressed," Philip explained to a Rhode Island official who wanted to keep the peace. "My father was then sachem, he relieved their distress in the most kind and hospitable manner. He gave them land to plant and build upon . . . they flourished and increased. By various means they got possession of a great part of his territory. But he still remained their friend till he died. My elder brother became sachem. . . . He was seized and confined and thereby thrown into illness and died. Soon after I became sachem, they disarmed all my people . . . their land was taken. But a small part of the dominion of my ancestors remains. I am determined not to live until I have no country."

The four years preceding the war were tense. "So the English were afraid and Philip was afraid, and both increased arms," said one contemporary account. The English feared that Philip was conspiring with other sachems to start a war. A Christian Indian minister, John

Sassamon, had reported a conspiracy to the governor of Plymouth Colony. (His warning was ignored.) Sassamon had been an advisor to Philip, but was now a rival. A week later Sassamon was found dead, floating under the ice on a pond. The authorities in Plymouth interviewed Philip and "many Indians," before charging three of Philip's chief counselors in a Plymouth court. They were convicted and hanged. (One survived his hanging and was shot a month later.) This is the incident that set off the war.

Philip struck within weeks of the trial, on June 24, 1675, and in the following months, Indians attacked and burned many towns: Middleborough, Dartmouth, Plymouth, Mendon, Brookfield, Springfield, Northampton, Lancaster, Medfield, Groton, Marlboro, Sudbury, Chelmsford, Worcester, Deerfield, Northfield, and other towns in Massachusetts. So many settlers evacuated the Connecticut River Valley that the militia commander forbade anyone else to leave. In Rhode Island, Providence, Warwick, Wickford, and Pawtuxet were destroyed. By February 1676, Indians were attacking within ten miles of Boston, and it looked as if the English would have to retreat to a few fortified seacoast towns.

The colonists were terrified, fearing a united Indian uprising. But native people were divided. Some of the Wampanoag, Nipmuc, and Poctumtuck joined Philip's company, carrying their own grievances from mistreatment and displacement. The Wampanoag on Cape Cod stayed outside the fight, as did the Christian Indians. At the start, the powerful Narragansett were not in the war. The Mohegan Indians, and later some Narraganasett, fought alongside the English. The colonists did not start winning the war until they adopted Indian tactics and were tipped off by their native allies about King Philip's whereabouts.

The Indians and English lived close to one another. For six decades leading up to the conflict, they lived with each other in trust and mistrust, trade and treaty, intermarriage and taboo, war and peace, tolerance and intolerance. Their worlds were interwoven in ways that are hard to know today. As a sachem, Metacom had taken a second name of Philip to better deal with the English. "By 1675 many Indians and English people had tried to merge their futures and needed one another for their communities to persist," writes historian James D. Drake in *King Philip's War*. "Indian and English polities had so intermeshed that in killing one another in King Philip's War they destroyed a part of themselves." Drake sees it as a civil war.

The Indians were too close, a daily reminder that threatened the Puritans, who believed they had been chosen to found an "English Israel" on "land the Lord God of Our Fathers hath given us for rightful possession." They feared becoming Indians. Some New Englanders saw themselves as fighting a holy war against barbarians, "the perfect children of the devil," one Puritan minister wrote. These two threads run through contemporary accounts of the war: the proximity of these two worlds and the Puritans' vehemence. ("These Heathens being like Wolves and other Beasts of Prey, that commonly do their Mischiefs in the Night, or by Stealth, durst not come out of the Woods and Swamps, where they lay skulking in small Companies," is a typical passage of a history published toward the war's end.)

In fourteen months the war was over. The English had begun to attack the Indians' food supplies and camps. Turner's attack had ended the Indians' war in the Connecticut River Valley. "If Philip's forces had been better supplied and had not had to fight three wars at once—one with the English; one with their Pequot, Mohegan, and Christian Indian allies; and one with the Mohawks—the colonists might well have lost everything. And they knew it," writes historian Jill Lepore in *The Name of War*.

King Philip was killed in August 1676. He was shot by Alderman, the Indian guide who led Captain Benjamin Church and his troops to a swamp near Philip's home in Mount Hope, Rhode Island. Church declared Philip "a doleful, great, naked, dirty beast" and ordered him to be quartered and hung from the trees. "For as much as he has caused many a Pilgrim to lie above ground, unburied, to rot, not one of his bones shall be buried," Church said.

Increase Mather, the Puritan minister of Boston, rejoiced at the news. "Immediately upon which a bullet took him in the head, and dashed out his brains, sending his cursed soul in a moment among the devils and blasphemers in hell forever," Mather wrote in his history of the war. "Nor could they, the Pilgrims, cease crying to the Lord against Philip until they had prayed a bullet through his heart."

Church marched to Plymouth with Philip's head. His arrival on August 13 was marked as a day of thanksgiving, a declared day of prayer. They put King Philip's head on a tall pole and left it there for decades.

The war had laid waste to New England. The Indians who had allied against the English suffered the worst causalities—losing the greatest proportion of their population—of any war fought on American territory. Nearly seventy percent of the Wampanoag, Nipmuc, Niantic, and Narragansett people in southeastern New England were killed or fled as refugees. Native prisoners of war were forced into servitude in English households or sold into slavery in the Caribbean. King Philip's nine-year-old son was sold as a slave. ("Philips boy goes now to be sold," Reverend John Cotton noted in a postscript to a letter.) At the war's end there were public executions of Indians in Boston. But the Indians who had helped the English were punished, too: They lost land and liberty. About four hundred "praying Indians," most of whom had tried to remain neutral, were rounded up during the war and imprisoned on barren Deer Island in Boston Harbor in winter. Hundreds starved or died of exposure. After the war, some of these non-combatants were also sold as slaves. The Puritans said that they couldn't tell heathen Indians from Christian Indians.

The colonists suffered for a century: One in sixteen men of military age was killed, half the towns were ruined and the economy was hobbled. "Per-capita incomes in New England did not recover their 1675 levels until 1775. They did not exceed the pre-1676 norm until after 1815," writes historian Stephen Saunders Webb in *1676: The End of American Independence*. Population did increase tenfold, but "these children of the Puritans, however, started from scratch and 'scratch' was not what it had it been before 1676. A large share of the capital of the Puritan fathers, the investments of their all by the colonizing generations of New England, had been consumed in the fires of King Philip's War." New England would be dependent on England for a century. After the war, English and Irish churches sent ships with relief aid.

This is only a brief summary. It cannot convey the pain inflicted by this complex war any more than a road map can convey a true sense of the land. The effects of this war last to this day. "King Philip's War remains the great watershed. Like the Civil War . . . it is difficult to escape the shadow it casts," writes historian Colin Calloway. "After the war, things were never the same again." Before the war, one in four New Englanders was an Indian. After their defeat, and increasing English immigration, Indians made up only one-tenth of the total population, and their political power was marginal. Barbara Tuchman calls World War I, "a path burnt across history." The same phrase could serve for King Philip's War.

II. The Place Where the Water Falls

A week before King Philip was killed, his trusted aid and sister-in-law, Weetamoo, drowned. Weetamoo was the sunksquaw (female chief, also known as the squaw sachem) of the Pocasset Wampanoag. She was an imposing figure. Mary Rowlandson, taken captive in the war, described her: "A severe, proud Dame she was, bestowing every day in dressing herself neat as much time as any of the Gentry of the land; powdering her hair, and painting her face, going with Necklaces, with Jewels in her ears, and Bracelets upon her hand." The English saw her as a threat, second only to King Philip. "She is as potent a prince as any round about her, and has as much corn, land, and men [as King Philip] at her command," said one report.

In a swamp near Taunton, Massachusetts, Weetamoo and a band of twenty-six warriors were surprised by twenty men from Taunton. Weetamoo escaped. She tried to swim, or raft, across the Taunton River and drowned. The English found her body alongshore and mutilated her. She was stripped of her necklaces and jewels and decapitated. Her head was placed on a pole and paraded around Taunton. "The Indians who were prisoners there knew it presently, and made a most horrid and diabolical lamentation, crying that it was their Queen's head," wrote Mather. Her head was displayed on the Taunton village green for twenty years.

Three hundred and twenty-five years later, three native women stood looking across the river to where Weetamoo's body had been found: Marge Bruchac, an Abenaki historian and storyteller; Nancy Eldredge, a Penobscot and Wampanoag educator; and Linda Coombs, an Aquinnah Wampanoag, who is the director of the Wampanoag Indigenous Program at Plimoth Plantation.

They talked about Weetamoo, and when they came to her death, they fell silent. There was only the sound of the wind. They looked across the river, then looked in different directions. "It sure is a sorrowful place," Nancy said. It was a moment infused with spirit. There were tears in Marge's eyes. She said something about how sad it was, but the wind carried her words away.

This is a scene from a film that was never finished. This fragment is all that exists: Three women in sorrow standing in the wind. We are not rescued from looking on this grief by the polish of a finished production: by a narrator taking us by the hand, by music massaging us, by the reassuring flow of a narrative. It's as if we had come upon the scene of a murder just moments later. This is an intensely private moment, but it is also a way to begin understanding the years since King Philip lost the war.

"A lot of New Englanders think that the Indians should have all vanished after King Philip's War. They still think that," one of those women, Marge Bruchac, told me early in my education about the war. "It was a terrible thing. Huge numbers of people were killed or sold into slavery. But we didn't disappear. And New Englanders still haven't quite come to terms with that."

I first met Marge years ago at Old Sturbridge Village, a living history museum, where she portrayed an Indian doctress. These healers were once ubiquitous, but are nearly invisible in official histories. With careful research Marge had created a composite character, Molly Geet (from the Abenaki for Margaret, *Mal-ga-leet*). An Indian doctoress "walked in two worlds" healing natives and whites, and Molly Geet's clothing mixed both worlds. Molly wore a man's tall hat with a green silk ribbon and a few feathers over her long, unbound, jet-black hair; a short gown and heavy cotton-lined petticoat held up with an Indian hand-woven belt; a blanket over her shoulders, a neck cloth, a silver brooch and earrings; and men's shoes. She carried a basket under one arm.

As this tall woman in a tall hat stood on the common, people approached her warily. They stopped six feet away and looked at her—from her tall hat to her dress, then back up and down again. They got a look as if they had just tasted something a little bitter. They wanted to ask: *What* are you? But they were too polite.

Once a crowd gathered, Molly/Marge began to tell a story. By midway into her first one she had won them over, and she drew them closer with each story she told. They relaxed. She has an uncanny talent to make people feel welcome and then tell them difficult truths. She would show them the plants she used for healing—wintergreen, pipsissewa, sweet fern, sassafras, burdock—finding them as she walked. But she was really imparting a native worldview to them, getting them to see a hidden history. Each plant opened up a view of society in the 1830s, bringing her listeners inside the houses of the whites to reveal how much they depended on the native healers, and how they shunned them. If "Yankee Prejudices" had been presented as a lecture, many people wouldn't sit for it, but as Molly, telling the story of a pine tree, or gossiping about how the minister's wife didn't like "injuns" in her house, she flew right in under the radar. She was gently subversive. "My primary goal is to doctor people's misperceptions," she said. Her husband calls her "the velvet hammer."

Marge's storytelling has been honored by other native storytellers. She has traveled Europe singing and telling stories. She teaches anthroplogy at the University of Connecticut and consults for New England museums and native communities. She has worked on identifying native remains held by colleges for proper reburial. I have seen her tell stories and lecture many times since, to teachers, Elderhostel groups, at conferences, and each time I marvel at her spirit. There's a nobility about her. Like the Indian doctress, she, too, walks in two worlds, the Abenaki and the prevailing culture. She walks with her ancestors and honors her ancestors in how she acts today. She walks with a sense of history.

When she was growing up in upstate New York in the 1950s, she was told that there were no Indians left in the state. The Indians were gone, a dead race. That was the official line taught in schools. Her grandfather and mother denied that they were Indians. It was a time when native people knew they had to be quiet about their heritage. One of her grandfather's brothers was killed by vigilantes; another brother had his sawmill burned down by his neighbors. Her grandfather was dark-skinned and said he was black. This was near Saratoga Springs, where there were many black stable hands. It was acceptable for blacks to work with horses, but not always for Indians.

Two of her grandfather's sisters were put in institutions and sterilized. They were just taken away. New York and Vermont had eugenics programs to "purify" the population. Vermont passed a sterilization law in 1931 and funded and arranged sterilizations until the early 1960s. Indians, blacks, and poor, rural, mixed-blood people were targeted.

Marge recently found an essay she wrote when she was eleven years old. It's about the Indians of upstate New York and the St. Lawrence Valley. The essay begins: "Along the river grow countless forests of cedar, spruce, fir, evergreens and hardwoods. Countless furred animals inhabit these forests. There is still one more creature . . . the Indian. The Indian still lives in the Stone Age." Then she read about the colonists, the French fur traders, and the French and Indian War. She was impressed by what this eleven-year-old knew. Then she came to the last sentence: "And the Indians have ceased to exist."

She could pound her listeners with the crimes of the past and confront them with their own ignorance. But Marge, like Molly Geet, is devoted to healing. And Molly has been her teacher and healer.

Marge was in a terrible auto accident some years ago. She had a brain stem injury and had to lie in a dark room for weeks, unable to filter out any sensation—light, sound, heat. She remembered being Molly Geet but not Marge Bruchac. The doctors were divided and kept ordering more tests. Some prescribed heavy medication, some urged institutionalization, but the doctors who knew her best told her to go back to performing as soon as possible and let Molly Geet take over.

She was shaky at first, but she says, "Whenever I got a little uncertain of what to do, I just let Molly tell me what to do." She would go perform, be Molly, return home and collapse. It bought her time to sort herself out—her mind was like a library in which all the books had been knocked off the shelves.

The brain injury was an ordeal that freed her. She had experiences known to people in altered states, or to those fasting and praying. "It's just that kind of disconnect between the part of the brain that's always filtering what to say, what to do, how to plan things out, and the part that's just intuitive, and just knows what to do next." She looks back on the accident as "an odd kind of gift." When she tells stories or lectures now, she relies on her intuition even more. "I'm always listening for what's the right thing—and the answers always come."

An earlier serious injury had set her on the path to storytelling. "Traditionally the people who did healing had been through something that was a breaking experience, some breaking of the spirit. I look at the things I've been through and all of these were temperings," she says. In her mid-twenties her right hand was nearly severed in an accident. She was fortunate to be taken to a university hospital that was pioneering microsurgery, otherwise her hand would have been amputated. She was in surgery nearly six hours and almost died. "On the table I was gone. I was way gone. One of the nurses that was there called me back," she says.

It was a year before she could do anything with her hand and several years before she could move the fingers independently. As part of her therapy she began to draw, a skill she had but never pursued. "And I learned that with this damaged hand I was really good at fine detail work because I could keep my hand in a rigid position for hours upon hours." She got a degree in commercial art and found freelance work in advertising design and public relations. Her work gave her insight into the power of persuasive storytelling. She brought this insight to her passion for historical reenacting and saw how the telling of history could shape people's perceptions.

She began telling traditional Abenaki stories and giving historical lectures in her late thirties, but it was quite a few years before she knew that "this was what I was put here to do." She recalls one moment of transformation: She was singing with her brother and nephews. They were performing at Odanak, a traditional Abenaki reserve in Quebec. The stage is outdoors in a small natural amphitheater by a river. Marge had been researching Molly Ockett, an Abenaki healer. A tune had come to her about Molly Ockett and she had "wrapped words around it." Everyone urged her to sing it. When she came to the song's last line—"I've searched through the hills and I've read all the words. Now I reach across time to take hold of your hands."—she held out her hands. "And I had that feeling that something took my hands and reached back. So even though it was a metaphorical statement in a song, it was a very real, tangible feeling at that moment." Right then she knew.

A long line of native women was waiting for her when she finished. "And as I stepped off the stage, each one of these women came forward and just embraced me. One after another after another. And tears were just streaming down their faces. And I had the sense that we all knew at that moment in time that this was what I had been given to carry."

"The stories need flesh and blood to walk around," the elders told her.

This history, of her people and herself, makes her a powerful storyteller and an insightful historian. In one talk she said, "As someone who's been broken and healed again, who dances on the edge between past and present, you've got a lot more responsibility than most people."

Marge Bruchac walks between two worlds, dances between the past and present. I asked her to walk me through Turners Falls.

We meet at the Shady Glen Diner, a low building that seems to be only a half-story tall. At one end of the L-shaped room, the Red Sox are playing on the television. We sit around the corner. I tell Marge how this town spooked me on my first visit and ask her what she thinks about Turners Falls.

"When I talk about this place—it was Peskeompskut—the place where the water falls. It was a safe zone for millennia—one of the places where native groups from all over the region came together to fish. And there were certain sachems who monitored the fishing so everybody got access, everybody got what they needed. And it was a peace zone. It was understood that you didn't make war in one of the places where everybody needed the resource. The salmon fishing was something that humans can't control. You can control your maize crop, you can control your hunting to a certain degree, but you can't control fishing. It's a seasonal thing. Every year the fish come from the ocean, they come up the river, they go north to spawn, and the one time when they pass through here is when you can fish. That was such a huge, communal, peaceful activity that so many people depended on. The archeological record of it alone is thick all along the river here—there's a depth of four to five feet of mixed soil and fish bones. You can test it in the soil; archeologists have done that. There's no question that this was a rich, rich fishing area. But when that massacre happened, it was completely counter to everything this place had ever known.

"Native people came here in the spring of 1676 because it was fishing time. Because they were in the middle of a war with the English, because this was still Indian territory, there were no English living here. This was known as a place you could safely bring anybody, so refugees from Wampanoag, Narrangasett, Nipmuc territories came here, along with the Pocumtuck people that were here. So you have all these native people here thinking they're in a safe place and then that's where they get attacked." Her voice is calm, matter-of-fact.

"The English wanted to portray it as a battle, but it was four hundred or more old men, women, and children. Slaughtered. So I don't think a memory like that just goes away easy. And I think especially because the area was settled by the English within a few decades, there was never any putting that memory to rest.

"Personally I think there is resonance where terrible things happen. The landscape remembers. It's not just human memory. But

I think there's some kind of vibe, for lack of a better word, that just holds on. It kind of permeates the place.

"People talk about going to places like Dachau, or the other concentration camps, and it's not still happening, but, boy, for people who go there, it's still happening, it's never ended. When you go to a cemetery, what do you feel? These are just decaying bodies in the ground, but why do people feel that sense of dread? Is there some kind of bio-plasm that remains? Is there some spirit that remains, to some sense? I think there is.

"I don't like being here, quite honestly." Even though she lives only twenty miles from here and once worked in the town next door, she avoids Turners Falls. When I first suggested that we visit the town, she politely suggested other places.

"Is this akin to the feeling that you had at the site where Weetamoo was found?" I ask.

"It's similar," she says. "Weetamoo is poignant because here's a woman who was King Philip's right hand-man so to speak, who was very loved, very revered, very powerful. And here's her end: It's so tragic. And then what the English make of that end is to cut off her head and stick it on a pole in the center of the town of Taunton. That's a sense of violation." She pauses. "And something about here goes deeper than that. Because it's not just the people who died here in May of 1676. It's the people who had been here through generations, whose memories were destroyed, whose sense of peace was destroyed.

"It's also things like—Here's a tragic little statistic for you: Turners Falls has been one of the primary collecting spots for native skeletal remains for about 150 years. One of the primary spots. As early as the 1840s, the American Antiquarian Society was sending people here to dig up native remains. It was known that this was where you could find them. Every spring people would go out to look for Indian skulls. Once a site was found, dozens of town's people would go there and sell and exchange and trade, and this stuff would go everywhere." Indian remains were a major Turner Falls export "Barrels of bones" were distributed among the local museums and colleges. When Route 2 was constructed above the falls, native remains were mixed in with the fill that went into the road.

In Native American belief it is important not to disturb burials because part of the spirit remains with the body. "The ancestors never really leave, but they go through a period of time when they travel away and after a year or so of travelling, then they're ready again because now they know what it's like in the spirit world. And if you need their help you can call on them."

She sums it up. "First you've got that desecration of a sacred site. Then you've got that devastating death, and then you've got that ongoing desecration of the dead and no coming to terms with it." She mentions some efforts to tell native history that "face a stiff resistance from many people who live here because they don't want to *think* about Indians. That's over. That's done. They just want to pick up those artifacts and put them on their mantelpiece and be done with it. It's almost like trophy collecting."

We finish our lunch and then tour Turner Falls and the town of Gill on the opposite bank, where many historians believe the massacre actually took place. We look at a granite monument to Captain Turner and his men. In the 1970s, activists from the American Indian Movement periodically painted it red, symbolically dipping Captain Turner in blood. Behind the monument we follow Riverview Drive. There's a small green park and a broad view of the river.

"Even though this is where I believe the massacre happened, this side here feels different," says Marge. "Isn't this beautiful?"

We drive back across the bridge into Turners Falls again and drive along the river on the other side by Unity Park. "This is where things feel very troubled to me. I get this sense in the pit of my stomach," she says. I agree with her that it doesn't seem right. "And yet there's the park, there's the kids playing," she says. It's a pretty park with good-size trees and a big playground. It would be a good example to use in a city-planning textbook.

We continue uphill and look at the houses on top built by the well-to-do in the late 19th century, and then drive downhill. Within a few blocks we are among the poor. Turners Falls has high rates of poverty, suicide, and spousal abuse.

Turners Falls was supposed to be a big mill city, another Lowell. After the Civil War, an industrialist dammed the falls to power mills, changing the river's run. An earlier dam in 1798 had completely destroyed the salmon's upstream run; within fifteen years salmon were rare in the Connecticut River. He had a city laid out, with a central avenue one hundred feet wide, and sold mill sites. Paper and cotton mills set up shop, and in the usual pattern, immigrants—French Canadian, Polish, German, and Irish—found work. By the start of the 20th century, the place was humming. The trolley from Greenfield ran along Avenue A past the Grand Trunk Hotel and an opera house that seated one thousand for vaudeville. The town was also the endpoint for log drives down the Connecticut. When the log drivers arrived, it was a wide-open town known for drinking and brawling. But Turners Falls was never as big as Lowell, never as big as it was planned to be, and it faded through most of the 20th century as the mills failed. The town looks a little like a fat man who has lost a hundred pounds and is still wearing the same pants.

On Seventh Street, we stop in front of a Catholic church. Catholic churches that once served the immigrants and their children are being closed. "They'll have to go to St. Mary's in Greenfield. It's really going to rip this town apart," says Marge.

Around the corner from the church, on Avenue A, is a war memorial. There's a tally board showing the dead and wounded in Iraq and Afghanistan. More than one thousand small flags have been set out, one for each death.

"The spirit of the town is there," she says, referring to the little flags. "And yet with virtually no understanding or knowledge of any deeper history."

Turners Falls High School is the "Home of the Indians." The high school teams are called the "Indians" and they have a mascot of an Indian head in a feather headdress. The school teaches very little about native history. A few good teachers try, but they meet a lot of resistance. Most schools claim that they are honoring native people by using them as mascots. But they don't say that in Turners Falls. They say that they have replaced the Indians. "They claim that they are now the Indians of Turners Falls. So they see it as a kind of transmutation. They live here: They're the Indians," says Marge. "And of course, ironically, many of the students at Turners Falls do have native ancestry, but they don't talk about it. Because the racism is so profound that admitting to being Indian is worse than being white and going native. That's akin to saying you were an Indian lover, or somebody in your ancestry was an Indian lover, literally."

There's a long, dishonorable tradition of white people playing Indians. Locally, this took the form of "The Independent Order of Scalpers," a fraternal lodge founded by three young men in 1893, which was still going strong in the 1950s. "With blood-curdling war-whoops and snake dances from the Highlands to the lake shore, the Scalpers both before and after the turn of the century celebrated holidays during the warmer months with revelry and merrymaking unsurpassed," reports the town's bicentennial program in 1954. The Scalpers had a lodge and a band with more than forty members in one photo, some dressed as Indians. Another photo shows three members wearing robes and headdresses, in front of a tipi, as Sitting Bull, Grey Eagle, and Big Owl.

"It's a conqueror culture," Marge says. She tells me to read a locally popular historical novel, *The Courage of Conviction*, which was published in 2001. "It's a heroic tale of Captain Turner. And it turns him into this dramatic hero of the colonial era." The book makes the massacre out to be Turner's great act of destiny. "And that's what made this a great valley, and that's what made him a great man."

We sit a moment looking at the flags and the tally board. "Look at the wounded," says Marge. There are more than 14,000. "That's the one that nobody's thinking of. The wounded are what we're going to be dealing with for decades now. Those are the people that are going to come home broken."

"Wars really don't end," I say. "Even though people want the soldiers to come home, take a shower, have a week off and go get a job. It's not quite the way it goes. No one wants to reckon with the aftermath, today, or after King Philip's War."

"So, after 1676, the veterans of King Philip's War are the ones who move into the areas where Indian massacres happened," she says. "You've got white folks who know full well they can't build that house until they kill off the Indians that live there. They can't settle that land. They can't plow those fields until the Indians are gone. The whole narrative of New England is about clearing out the Indians to make way for the English to move in. So imagine what kind of resonance that creates over time."

We return to the diner and sit out front. Marge is sad, as sad as she appeared when she visited the site where Weetamoo was found. Her usual quick-fire intelligence is subdued. This visit has depressed her, she says. It has depressed me, both the history and the thought that I put her through this. She needs to leave. I ask her one more question.

"So King Philip's War ended 330 years ago—"

"I don't think it's ended."

"Really?"

"Uh-huh."

"You don't think it's ended?"

"No," she says softly. "And I think that's part of what you sense when you're here. The war didn't just float through here and move on somewhere else. Some part of it got stuck here."

"Does that happen with all wars?"

"I don't know. Look at what's happening in Vietnam now: You've got veterans from the U.S. going back to find MIAs. And you've got Vietnamese people who are helping them. That's a real resolution. Look at what's happening at the commemorations at Nagasaki and Hiroshima, where people are pulling together boxes of ashes and trying to make peace. You know, I think in places where people are consciously trying to overcome, or to move past, or move through, the resonance of war, that there's a chance of leaving it behind and moving on. But I think in places where people haven't dealt with it, that's where it sticks.

"There's something going on in the ground under our feet that held the imprints of all those moccasins. That supported all those communities. Those fish bones that mix in the soil and make it rich. And now it's just silt that washes into the river. But before it would have been something that would have helped things to grow. So in a way it's almost like the soil here is rotten."

"Rotten?"

"Yeah. It's like the soil and the spirit here is rotten. Because it started to decay, but it hasn't grown anything positive. I mean that's a pretty broad statement. I'm sure there are positive things going on all the time. I don't mean to kind of wash over it with that big brush. But that may be a big part of the problem. Maybe that's how places where death and destruction happen get stuck in time.

"I mean, jeez, why else would people go to such enormous efforts to find the shards of bone from MIAs? It's military, routine practice to find every little missing piece. But yet if I go to a museum and say I think you might have a bone shard from someone who died at Turners Falls, they'll say, 'We have hundreds of bone shards. What does it matter?'"

Turners Falls is divorced from deep time, from the true history of the land. For thousands of years this place kept time by the salmon leaping the falls and the Indians gathering to fish. In an instant on one spring morning in 1676, that ended. In another instant, the falls were dammed; the salmon were gone. The river's run has changed; time has changed. The Indian heritage is denied. What I had felt on my first visit was the pain of divorce.

After Marge left, I was drawn back to the Gill side of the river, to what is probably the massacre site. I saw a man talking to some boys who were fishing. I got out of my car to talk to him. He was chasing the boys off his three hundred feet of river frontage—his house is right across the road, facing the river. I asked him if he knew where the massacre of the Indians took place.

"The Indian massacre? That's up by the lights," he said. He directed me to the traffic light by the bridge and told me to go up the hill about two or three miles.

"To tell the truth," he said, "there were a lot of whites that got massacred, too."

"There were?" I asked.

"That's what I think," he said.

He gave me the directions again. I left town.

One time Marge went to Plimoth Plantation. The museum there is devoted to telling the story of 17th-century interactions between the English and Wampanoag. She was meeting with Nancy Eldredge, a Penobscot-Wampanoag who was then education director for the museum's Wampanoag Indigenous Program. Marge wanted to stop at a drugstore.

"I can't go in that drugstore," said Nancy.

"Why?" asked Marge. "It's just a drugstore."

"That's where King Philip's head was," said Nancy.

III. The Place Where People Grow Corn

Up the river a half-dozen miles, in another season, I go to hear Marge talk at a church in Northfield, Massachusetts. Northfield on a cold and quiet Sunday morning in November is a poised and gracious town. The houses and churches stand back from the wide Main Street with the kind of self-assurance that makes drivers just off the interstate slow down and look. Northfield looks like home—the kind of home many crave: small-town, stable, and knowable. It is a home built on someone else's home.

Marge Bruchac's Abenaki ancestors burned Northfield four times. Four years before King Philip's War, in 1671, some of the colonists claimed that the Sokoki, the southernmost band of Abenaki, had sold and abandoned the land called Squakheag on the English maps. The Sokoki had not left and made that clear: The English were forced to flee Northfield twice—once during King Philip's War. An English town was delayed for forty years.

For thousands of years Squakheag was a council ground for the Abenaki, Pocumtuck, and other native peoples to gather. Reading the historical markers around town, you learn that some Indians were once here, but they appear only as an impediment to progress. Coming into town by the Northfield Mount Hermon School, there's a four-foot-tall obelisk, inscribed:

Nathaniel Dickinson
Was killed
And scalped
By the Indians
At this place.
April 15, 1747
Aged 48.

No one would want to put up a sign that says: We have taken this place from others. American history begins by resisting this truth. Yet that is why Marge is here this morning, and why she will return. There are other ways to put up historical markers. Just being here is a start, a living Abenaki, proof against the belief that your people are extinct.

"And grace will lead me home," Marge sings as she stands facing the congregation of the First Parish Unitarian Church. On this morning, two weeks before Thanksgiving, the small flock is tentative in its singing of *Amazing Grace*. "When we've been there 10,000 years, bright shining as the sun," she sings and smiles to herself. When Marge smiles like that, she's about to tell you something important.

She greets us and thanks us for the chance to bring her people's stories back home to Squakheag. "There are many names for it. We say, 'at the place where people grow corn.' Beside that long river, that Quinn-ecti-cook river," she sounds out the name that gave rise to Connecticut, "that flows from the north to the south and all along that place is where my ancestors have always lived.

"Stories are not just for the living," she says, and speaks Abenaki for her ancestors. As she tells her stories, she mixes in her native language. She picks up braided sweetgrass from a table, lights it with a candle, and draws the smoke near her with a sweep of her arm. The smoke carries our world, she says. "It may seem that this room is empty, but my ancestors are present."

"I must also thank all other creatures, for they listen. The *awaasak*, the four-legged ones; *namasak*, the ones listening beneath the waves. The *sipsak*, winged ones." She continues in Abenaki and returns to English. "I also thank, for listening to these stories and songs, the ones whose roots are deep in the ground and arms are reaching into the sky. All the *abaziak*, the tree people. I also thank the *alakwasak*, the sky people: the sun, the moon, and the stars.... You're lucky. Because if I were to do this proper, I'd keep you here all day and into the night and on to the next morning, thanking all the creatures by name," Marge says. "For the Abenaki, we can wrap it up by thanking all my relations, *miziwi*, for listening to these stories.

"The story I would like to share with you is one I can tell only after the frost has hit the ground. And when that frost comes is when we tell the oldest of our stories. The stories go back 10,000 years or more. And I was thinking to myself and chuckling because I've never sung *Amazing Grace* and thought about that phrase: *10,000 years*. We've already been here 10,000 years."

In the oldest story told by the western Abenaki, Odzihozo shapes himself out of the leftover dust of creation. At first this dust creature has no nose or mouth. Seven times Tabaldak, who shaped the other creatures, sends down lightning, making two eyes to see what is close and far away, two nostrils for sweet and sour, two ears to hear both sides of an argument, and one mouth, so the creature speaks only half as much as it listens. Then Odzihozo, this giant, pushes the earth aside, making mountains, and stands up. "Years go by. Many seasons change. Waters come out of the sky and flow down those great big mountains. . . . That place where Odzihozo sat fills up with water in the shape of a long narrow lake. Hundreds of years pass, and then thousands.

"Strange people come. They walk around and name everything they see after themselves and the places they came from. They name one place New Netherlands. Another one New France. New England. They name them by these crazy names. And one of them, seeing this place, he names it after himself. You know that place?" Marge asks, referring to the long lake. "They named it Lake Champlain. And all the Abenakis, we laughed. For anyone in his right mind knows that is Bitownbauk, that is the place in between the mountains, that is the place where Odzihozo shaped himself. It is the place we come from. And that is one of our stories."

The ancient Abenaki stories have a vibrancy that outshines the hymnal. People lean toward her. These stories can be entertainment or a lesson, she says. "It can also be a way to explain that what I have to share with you, although a very old, traditional story, is not a game or a rumor that passes from one to another and changes with every telling. It has a shape and a form that is very specific. And people often forget that about our oral tradition." If she were to tell this story with Abenaki elders in the room, she would be told, "You must not forget this piece; you must not forget the shape of this."

If a geologist were telling the story, he would tell us how 10,000 years ago, when the ice receded, it formed a long narrow lake. If an archaeologist was the guest, she would tell us about the spear points, stones used for boiling, and the evidence of wigwams found in a 10,000-year-old hunting camp by that long lake.

"Ten thousand years of continuous occupation in one place: this isn't a novel practice—some generations go by and you lose something and then you find it again. And most of the Jewish people I know talk in the same way about Jewish traditions. They say it's about that continuous survival and continuous rejuvenating of the tradition," Marge says. From Turners Falls to Northfield, we had traveled a short distance, only a few miles up that long river's valley, but the view had opened to a different time scale. In Turners Falls we had stared at a divide from the time before. In Northfield we talked of 10,000 years.

"The last four hundred years are the smallest part of our history, probably the most devastating, but also the smallest," she says. "This is all really new. And hell, if we could live through an Ice Age, we could live through European invasion.

"Understand the physical and mental and emotional and spiritual skill it takes to have survived everything that came at us. Imagine that we were thrown in the water, and we've surfaced. And people are going, what are you doing surfacing? We threw you in the water!

You're supposed to drown down there! But we learned to swim. And sometimes I feel that is just incomprehensible to many non-native people. Sometimes I feel like we have to justify our ability to adapt. Whereas if you read our old stories and you hear our old traditions, it's no big surprise. It's what we've always been doing."

If you were to look only at just the last four hundred years, you would miss the continuum of native history, the way the ancient past shapes today. You would have been misled by placing event after event on a timeline. "What I see happening in modern American culture is that the time focus is so narrow. I mean four hundred years is like that"—she snaps her fingers—"in the broad span of time. So much effort is expended on saying native people are gone or that everything is lost. When in fact it's seasonal. But if your seasons span fifty or a hundred years instead of a few months, it's a different perspective. When you think back over deep time, this could have been going on for millennia that things get lost and things get found."

Traditionally, many indigenous communities see time as a spiral. The past is never far away. Performing a ritual, "you're literally calling the ancestors in with you, you literally bring stories out of dreamtime into the present, you find ways to cut through time to make things part of where we are now," Marge says. "And if you think about it, Christians believe the same thing. Why else would you eat the blood and body of Christ?" It is a way of having "time travel to meet you." Contemporary Indians have updated this belief, she says. "There are some native intellectuals who say that time is sort of like the DNA strand. That it's woven and twists on itself. There's communication between all the different parts of it, and you can pull out one part, but it's useless without all the other connecting links."

Many times Marge has stood before a blackboard in a schoolroom and said, "Here's how Europeans think of time." She draws a straight line. Then she says, "Here's how native people think of time." She draws a curving trail of light like the sun's path across the sky. She pauses and then says, "but here's how native people *really* think of time." She starts drawing a line that looks like the double helix of DNA, or like many light waves, each at a different frequency. The lines layer; they braid together. It looks like the Mohegan Trail of Life, the weave that shows that they are always going back and forth on the same road. She turns from the board: "So I can say to you, the past is right here in the room with us, and the future is there, too, but if we don't have any way of seeing it, then all we see is a tangled line. But if we have a philosophy that allows us to understand how that tangled line opens itself up into a very clear shape, it's no longer a source of confusion; it's a source of connection."

I think of the story of Odzihozo creating that long lake and I ask her, "What is the shape of 10,000 years?"

"The 10,000 past or the 10,000 to come?" she replies. "We're at a hinge point. We're in between two very large eras." One large era was before colonization and the other is colonization that has not ended, she says. Native nations are in a constant struggle for rights and sovereignty. Some activists want to fight, but Marge thinks there's still time to teach people. "This is a wonderful time of resurgence. This is a time when it all begins to come back together." There is a renaissance of native storytellers, writers, singers, dancers, and revived languages. The Wampanoag language is a great example. Thought to be lost, it has been restored by working with the Bibles translated by Indians in the 1600s. "Things are changing in a remarkable way. For me it's an easy time to be hopeful. The next 10,000 years is when we learn how to continue to be native."

IV. Another Sunday

One Sunday in late October, I visit Stoddard, a New Hampshire hill town that was founded one hundred years after King Philip's War. A local historian begins an afternoon tour in the church with a short introduction to the town's history. Stoddard's population peaked at about 1,200 people in 1840 and fell rapidly. In 1930 there were only 113 inhabitants living amid rural ruins, the abandoned houses and farms of their absent neighbors. Bottle-making was a big industry, but the railroad never came to Stoddard, and by the 1870s the bottlers' demand for clear glass, instead of the local amber glass, killed the business. Lumber, cattle driving, and tourism followed. Today, Stoddard lives by the summer people drawn to its five lakes. The year-round population of 958 more than doubles in the summer.

We troop outside, a group of about twenty, mostly old folks, and walk up a steep hill to the old graveyard. Dark clouds have swept in. Sunlight hunts at the edges of the clouds, breaking through now and again. The maple trees are golden. Stoddard sits in Sunday quiet. It is as if the town has dwindled to twenty people. No one else is out. They are inside by a fire or a woodstove, rolled up in Sunday—newspapers, football games, family visits, family meetings over dining room tables with rows of bills, like soldiers on a parade ground. Where we stand there are layers of quiet. The "Rock of Ages" is a sedimentary rock, layer after layer of the not-living, falling to rest.

The graveyard is a powerful place. The land is a shaggy meadow, a rolling ocean, the graves athwart and tossed. Some of the tall, thin stones are pitching forward, others are heeling back or shifting side to side. The dead are at sea. The hillside falls away toward stone wall and old maples. There's a view to the hills. The ground is spongy.

We look at a few of the black slate gravestones decorated with willows and cherubs. One with seven arches on top tells of a family that lost seven children in the thirteen years from 1792 to 1805. The youngest lived "two hours" and the oldest, "four years, four months, four days." Another, with the stylized image of a boy and girl, tells of the loss of a brother and sister, ages four and two, who died within three days of each other in 1798.

It starts to drizzle, flecking the slate with dark spots. I miss my wife and our dog and want to go home. We are passing into the season of barren trees, when almost any house, illuminated from within, looks like a warm haven in a cold world. It is odd for us to be milling around an old graveyard in a chilly drizzle. Somewhere out there, American culture clatters like a pinball machine, like an arcade of cell phones, televisions, radios, and computers.

By our view, these dead we stand among are long dead. *Israel Towne died April 28, 1813. Mrs. Rhoda, wife of Captain Nathaniel Evans, died March 8, 1815.* Yet in the silence I felt the dead claiming us. What do the epitaphs and dates say? What do Levi Green and Enos Locke and Hannah Spaulding say to us? That they died only yesterday and we'll die tomorrow. The distinctions that we make between years and decades and centuries fall away. Time collapses in an old graveyard. We try to pretend otherwise, to build a wall between ourselves and the dead. We look at the dates and the bygone Old Testament names. Those people were practically another species, we think. But we are with them. We are their contemporaries. All of us are united by living in the years since King Philip's War.

In India there is a popular story from Sanskrit scripture about how time passes. Vishnu, the preserver of life, allows Narada to befriend him. Vishnu asks Narada to fetch him a drink of water. Narada goes forth and at the first door he knocks on, he meets a beautiful woman. He forgets his errand. They fall in love, marry, and have three children. After many years, Narada becomes the head of the household, tending the fields and the cattle. In his twelfth year in the village the monsoon rains are especially heavy. Narada's village is destroyed. In the flood, he struggles to hold on to his wife and children, but one by one they are swept from him, and he is washed back to Vishnu, who has been waiting for him. "Where is the water you went to fetch for me? I have been waiting more than half an hour." It had been but a wink of time.

Close to four hundred years have passed since King Philip's War. Other wars have followed, wars against the Abenaki, Tuscarora, Yamasee, Ottawa, Delaware, Seneca, Shawnee, Ojibwa, Wyandot, Potawtomi, Miami, British, Barbary Coast pirates, Creek, Seminole, Black Hawk, Navajo, Mexicans, Sioux, Ute, Apache, Nez Perce, Comanche, Kiowa, Southern Cheyenne, Arapaho, Nicaraguans, Spanish, Filipinos, Yaqui, Germans, Italians, Japanese, Koreans, Vietnamese, Cambodians, Laotians, Afghanistanis, Iraqis. The United States has been involved in civil wars, revolutions, cold wars, covert wars, wars by proxy, occupations, and interventions in Sumatra, Argentina, China, Samoa, Chile, Hawaii, Panama, Honduras, Dominican Republic, Cuba, Mexico, Yugoslavia, Turkey, Guatemala, El Salvador, Uruguay, Puerto Rico, Haiti, Greece, Congo, Ecuador, Peru, Brazil, Bolivia, Borneo, Jamaica, Venezuela, Costa Rica, Ghana, Angola, Lebanon, Grenada, Suriname, the Maldives, Liberia. The United States has plotted assassinations in Cuba, Iran, Korea, North Korea, India, Egypt, Indonesia, Iraq, Burundi, France, Zaire, Libya, Morocco, and Lebanon.

It has been the era of wars, as are all eras. It has been the era of steam, the era of the telegraph and railroad. It has been the Machine Age, the Atomic Age, the American Century, the Space Age, the Computer Age. The calendar has been crowded with inventions and seemingly important announcements, big news and headlines—all of it now compressed like newspapers at a landfill. Wonderful things were done; horrible things were done.

There were perhaps 10 million people living in North America in 1675. Today there are 450 million. There were about 500 million people in the world; today there are 6 billion.

See it like Vishnu. It is just a moment since King Philip's head was put on a pole. See it like a Wampanoag, like an Abenaki. Four hundred years is but a moment in 10,000 years. Time is curved, time is braided. Throw out your clocks.

Bibliography

Books About Time

Abe, Masao. *A Study of Dogen*. State University of New York Press, 1992.

Aciman, Andre. *False Papers*. Farrar, Straus and Giroux, 2000.

Aitken, Robert. *The Morning Star: New and Selected Zen Writings*. Shoemaker and Hoard, Publishers, 2003.

——. *A Zen Wave: Basho's Haiku and Zen*. Shoemaker and Hoard, Publishers, 2003.

Barbour, Julian. *The End of Time: The Next Revolution in Physics*. Oxford University Press, 1999.

Bennett, John, et al. *Uqalurait: An Oral History of Nunavut*. McGill Queens University Press, 2004.

Borges, Jorge Luis. *Labyrinths*. New Directions, 1964.

Brand, Stewart. *The Clock of the Long Now*. Basic Books, 1999.

Boorstin, Daniel J. *The Discoverers*. Random House, 1983.

Buckley, Jerome Hamilton. *The Triumph of Time: A Study of the Victorian Concepts of Time, History, Progress, and Decadence*. The Belknap Press of Harvard University Press, 1966.

Calder, Nigel. *Einstein's Universe*. The Viking Press, 1979.

Callahan, Steven. *Adrift: 76 Days Lost at Sea*. Houghton Mifflin, 1986.

Crosby, Alfred W. *The Measure of Reality: Quantification and Western Society, 1250–1600*. Cambridge University Press, 1997.

Davies, Paul. *About Time: Einstein's Unfinished Revolution*. Simon and Schuster, 1995.

——. *God and the New Physics*. Simon and Schuster, 1983.

Denby, David. *American Sucker*. Little, Brown and Co., 2004.

Deutsch, David. *The Fabric of Reality*. Penguin Books, 1997.

Draaisma, Douwe. *Metaphors of Memory: A History of Ideas About Mind*. Cambridge University Press, 2000.

Eberle, Gary. *Sacred Time and the Search for Meaning*. Shambhala, 2002.

Foster, Nelson, and Jack Shoemaker, eds. *The Roaring Stream: A New Zen Reader*. The Ecco Press, 1996.

Fraser, J. T. *Time: The Familiar Stranger*. University of Massachusetts Press, 1987.

——, ed. *The Voices of Time*. University of Massachusetts Press, 1981.

Galison, Peter. *Einstein's Clocks, Poincare's Maps: Empires of Time*. W.W. Norton and Company, 2003.

Greene, Brian. *The Fabric of the Cosmos*. Alfred A. Knopf, 2004.

Gorst, Martin. *Measuring Eternity: The Search for the Beginning of Time*. Broadway Books, 2001.

Griffiths, Jay. *A Sideways Look at Time*. Jeremy P. Tarcher/Putnam, 2002.

Grudin, Robert. *Time and the Art of Living*. Ticknor & Fields, 1982.

Hoskins, Janet. *The Play of Time: Kodi Perspectives on Calendars, History, and Exchange*. University of California Press, 1993.

Hyatt, Harry Middleton. *Folk-lore from Adams County, Illinois*. Memoirs of the Alma Egan Hyatt Foundation, 1965.

Kim, Hee-Jin. *Dogen Kigen, Mystical Realist*. The University of Arizona Press, 1975.

Kern, Stephen. *The Culture of Time and Space, 1880–1918*. Harvard University Press, 1983.

LaFleur, William R., ed. *Dogen Studies.* (Studies in East Asian Buddhism No. 2). University of Hawaii, 1985.

Le Goff, Jacques. *Time, Work and Culture in the Middle Ages.* The University of Chicago Press, 1980.

Levine, Robert. *A Geography of Time.* Basic Books, 1997.

Mishra, Pankaj. *An End to Suffering: The Buddha in the World.* Farrar, Straus and Giroux, 2004.

Morris, Taylor. *The Walk of the Conscious Ants.* Alfred A. Knopf, 1972.

Mussey, Barrows, ed. *Yankee Life by Those Who Lived It.* Alfred A. Knopf, 1947.

Needham, Joseph. *Time: The Refreshing River.* Macmillan, 1943.

Porter, Bill. *Road to Heaven: Encounters with Chinese Hermits.* Mercury House, 1993.

Quinones, Ricardo J. *The Renaissance Discovery of Time.* Harvard University Press, 1972.

Ridderbos, Katinka, ed. *Time.* Cambridge University Press, 2002.

Rotenberg, Robert. *Time and Order in Metropolitan Vienna: A Seizure of Schedules.* Smithsonian Institution Press, 1992.

Rybczynski, Witold. *Waiting for the Weekend.* Viking Press, 1991.

Schall, Jan, ed. *Tempus Fugit, Time Flies.* Nelson-Atkins Museum of Art, 2000.

Stombaugh, Joan. *Impermanence Is Buddha-nature: Dogen's Understanding of Temporality.* University of Hawaii Press, 1990.

Tanahashi, Kazuaki, ed. *Moon in a Dewdrop: Writings of Zen Master Dogen.* North Point Press, 1985.

Tharp, Twyla, with Mark Reiter. *The Creative Habit: Learn It and Use It for Life.* Simon and Schuster, 2003.

Visser, Margaret. *The Geometry of Love: Space, Time, Mystery and Meaning in an Ordinary Church.* North Point Press, 2001.

Whitrow, G. J. *Time in History.* Oxford University Press, 1989.

——. *What Is Time?* Thames and Hudson Ltd., 1972.

Young, Michael. *The Metronomic Society*. Harvard University Press, 1988.

Yourgrau, Palle. *A World Without Time: The Forgotten Legacy of Godel and Einstein*. Basic Books, 2004.

Timescape: *"Did But Little. Caught One Shad."*

Banks, William Nathaniel. "Temple, New Hampshire." *The Magazine Antiques*, October 1975.

Blood, Henry Ames. *The History of Temple, New Hampshire*. George C. Rand & Avery, 1860.

Bushman, Richard L. *The Refinement of America*. Alfred A. Knopf, 1992.

Butler, Jon. "Magic, Astrology and Early American Religious Heritage, 1600-1760." *American Historical Review*, Vol. 84, April 1979.

Bruegel, Martin. "'Time That Can Be Relied Upon.' The Evolution of Time Consciousness in the Mid-Hudson Valley, 1790–1860." *Journal of Social History*, Spring 1995.

Cole, Arthur H. "The Tempo of Mercantile Life in Colonial America." *Business History Review*, Autumn 1959.

Demos, John. *Circles and Lines: The Shape of Life in Early America*. Harvard University Press, 2004.

Featherstonhaugh, George William. *Excursion Through the Slave States, from Washington on the Potomac to the Frontier of Mexico: With Sketches of Popular Manners and Geological Notices*. 1844. Reprinted, Negro Universities Press, 1968.

Fischer, David Hackett. *Albion's Seed: Four British Folkways in America*. Oxford University Press, 1989.

Hall, David H. *Worlds of Wonder, Days of Judgment: Popular Religious Belief in Early New England*. Alfred A. Knopf, 1989.

Hensley, Paul B. "Time, Work, and Social Context in New England." *New England Quarterly*, December 1992.

Historical Society of Temple, New Hampshire. *A History of Temple, New Hampshire, 1768–1976*. W. L. Bauhan, 1976.

Kittredge, George Lyman. *The Old Farmer and His Almanack*. 1920. Reprinted: Benjamin Blom, Inc., 1967.

Landes, David S. *Revolution in Time: Clocks and the Making of the Modern World*. Belknap Press of Harvard University Press, 1983.

Larcom, Lucy. "Among Lowell Mill Girls: A Reminiscence." *The Atlantic Monthly*, November 1881.

O'Malley, Michael. *Keeping Watch: A History of American Time*. Viking, 1990.

Ruffin, J. Rixey. "'Urania's Dusky Veils:' Heliocentrism in Colonial Almanacs, 1700–1735." *New England Quarterly*, Vol. 70, No. 2, July 1997.

Sagendorph, Robb. *America and Her Almanacs*. Yankee, Inc., and Little, Brown and Company, 1970.

Stephens, Carlene F. *On Time: How America Has Learned to Live by the Clock*. Smithsonian Institution, National Museum of American History, and Little, Brown and Company, 2002.

Stowell, Marion Barber. *Early American Almanacs: The Colonial Weekday Bible*. Burt Franklin & Co., Inc., 1977.

Wenrick, Jon Stanley. *For Education and Entertainment—Almanacs in the Early American Republic, 1783–1815*. Ph.D. dissertation, Claremont Graduate School, 1974.

Winik, Daniel. "'Information of the Unlearned': The Enlightenment in Early American Almanacs, 1650-1800." *The Concord Review*, Vol. 12, 2001–2002.

The Continuous

Allen, Fred. *Much Ado About Me*. Little, Brown, and Company, 1956.

Allen, Robert C. "Contra the Chaser Theory," in *Film Before Griffith*. John L. Fell, ed. University of California Press, 1983.

Baker, George P. *The Formation of the New England Railroad Systems*. Harvard University Press, 1937.

Bel Geddes, Norman. *Miracle in the Evening: An Autobiography*. Doubleday and Co., 1960.

Brick, Michael. "And Next to the Bearded Lady, Premature Babies." *The New York Times*, June 12, 2005.

Browne, George Waldo. *The History of Hillsborough, New Hampshire 1735–1921*. John R. Clarke, Printers, 1922.

Burrows, Edwin G., and Mike Wallace. *Gotham: A History of New York City to 1898*. Oxford University Press, 1999.

Butsch, Richard. *The Making of American Audiences: From Stage to Television, 1750–1990*. Cambridge University Press, 2000.

Caffin, Caroline. *Vaudeville*. Mitchell Kennerley, 1914.

Christie, Ian. *The Last Machine: Early Cinema and the Birth of the Modern World*. BBC Education Developments, 1994.

Cleveland, Frederick A., and Fred Wilbur Powell. *Railroad Promotion and Capitalization in the United States*. 1909. Reprinted, Johnson Reprint Corporation, 1966.

Cressy, Will M. *Continuous Vaudeville*. Richard G. Badger, 1914.

Cronon, William. *Nature's Metropolis: Chicago and the Great West*. W.W. Norton & Co., 1991.

DiMeglio, John E. *Vaudeville U.S.A*. Bowling Green University Popular Press, 1973.

Dunbar, Seymour. *A History of Travel in America*. 1915. Reprinted, Greenwood Press, 1968.

Ely, James W. *Railroads and American Law*. University Press of Kansas, 2001.

Haddock, Charles B. *Addresses and Miscellaneous Writings*. Metcalf and Co., 1846.

Gopnik, Adam. "Metropolitan." *The New Yorker*, June 13 and 20, 2005.

Grau, Robert. *Forty Years Observation of Music and the Drama*. Broadway Publishing Company, 1909.

——. *The Stage in the 20th Century*. 1912. Reprinted Benjamin Blom, Inc., 1969.

Green, Abel, and Joe Laurie Jr. *Showbiz: From Vaude to Video*. Henry Holt & Co., 1951.

Harlow, Alvin F. *Steelways of New England*. Creative Age Press, Inc., 1946.

Howells, William Dean. *Imaginary Interviews*. Harper & Brothers, Publishers, 1910.

——. *Letters Home*. The Metropolitan Magazine Co., 1905.

Kasson, John F. *Rudeness and Civility: Manners in 19th Century America*. Hill and Wang, 1990.

King, Thomas Starr, ed. *The Railroad Jubilee*. J. H. Eastburn, City Printer, 1852.

Laurie, Joe Jr. *Vaudeville: From the Honky-Tonks to the Palace*. Henry Holt & Co., 1953.

Macy, John A. "The Career of the Joke." *The Atlantic Monthly*, October 1905.

Martin, Albro. *Railroads Triumphant*. Oxford University Press, 1992.

Meinig, D. W. *The Shaping of America. Continental America, 1800–1867,* Vol. 2, Yale University Press, 1993.

——. *The Shaping of America. Transcontinental America, 1850–1915*, Vol. 3, Yale University Press, 1998.

McLean, Albert F. Jr. *American Vaudeville as Ritual*. University of Kentucky Press, 1965.

———. "Genesis of Vaudeville: Two Letters from B. F. Keith." *Theatre Survey*, Vol. 1, 1960.

Marston, William Moulton, and John Henry Feller. *F. F. Proctor, Vaudeville Pioneer*. Richard R. Smith, 1943.

Marx, Harpo, with Rowland Barber. *Harpo Speaks!* Limelight Editions, 1985.

Musser, Charles. "Another Look at the 'Chaser Theory.'" *Studies in Visual Communication*, Fall 1984.

Page, Brett. *Writing for Vaudeville*. The Home Correspondence School, 1915.

Ripley, William Z. *Railroads, Rates and Regulations*. 1912. Reprinted, Arno Press, 1973.

Samuels, Charles, and Louise Samuels. *Once Upon a Stage*. Dodd, Mead & Co., 1974.

Sante, Luc. *Low Life*. Farrar, Straus & Giroux, 1991.

Schivelbusch, Wolfgang. *The Railway Journey*. Urizen Books, 1979.

Slide, Anthony. *The Encyclopedia of Vaudeville*. Greenwood Press, 1994.

Smith, Wilson. "Purity and Progress in New Hampshire: The Role of Charles B. Haddock." *The New England Quarterly*, December 1955.

Snyder, Robert W. *The Voice of the City: Vaudeville and Popular Culture in New York*. Oxford University Press, 1989.

Sobel, Bernard. *A Pictorial History of Vaudeville*. The Citadel Press, 1961.

Spitzer, Marian. *The Palace*. Atheneum, 1969.

Stein, Charles W., ed. *American Vaudeville As Seen by Its Contemporaries*. Alfred A. Knopf, 1984.

Stilgoe, John R. *Metropolitan Corridor: Railroads and the American Scene*. Yale University Press, 1983.

Vance, James E. Jr. *The North American Railroad*. The Johns Hopkins University Press, 1995.

Ward, James A. *Railroads and the Character of America, 1820–1887*. The University of Tennessee Press, 1986.

Ward, John William, ed. *Society, Manners, and Politics in the United States: Letters on North America by Michael Chevalier*. Peter Smith, 1967.

Timescape: *The Immortality of Property*

Boorstin, Daniel. *The Americans: The Democratic Experience*. Vintage Books, 1974.

Dodd, Edwin Merrick. *American Business Corporations until 1860*. Harvard University Press, 1954.

Friedman, Lawrence M. *A History of American Law*. Simon and Schuster, 1973.

Higginson, Henry Lee. "Justice to the Corporations." *The Atlantic Monthly*, January 1908.

Jaher, Frederic Cople, ed. *The Age of Industrialism in America*. The Free Press, 1968.

Levin, Leonard W. *The Law of the Commonwealth and Chief Justice Shaw*. Harvard University Press, 1957.

Trachtenberg, Alan. *The Incorporation of America: Culture and Society in the Gilded Age*. Hill & Wang, 1982.

Wright, Conrad Edick, and Katheryn P. Viens, eds. *Entrepreneurs: The Boston Business Community, 1700–1850*. Massachusetts Historical Society, 1997.

A Family History of Water

Allen, Everett S. *A Wind to Shake the World*. Little, Brown and Co., 1976.

Armstrong, John Borden. *Factory Under the Elms: A History of Harrisville, N.H. , 1774–1969*. Merrimack Valley Textile Museum/MIT Press, 1969.

Ballard, David. "Hurricane, Flames and Flood Leave Peterborough Scene of Devastation." *The Peterborough Transcript*, September 29, 1938.

Clark, Francelia, and Dave Robinson with Alison Rossiter. *Lake Nubanusit (Long Pond/Great Pond): Its History and People.* Nubanusit Lake Association, Inc., 2000.

Cantor, Norman F. *Imagining the Law: Common Law and the Foundations of the American Legal System*. HarperCollins Publishers, 1999.

Coffin. John E. *It Did Happen Here!* The Sentinel Publishing Company, 1938.

Colony, John, Sr. Interview with the author. December 16, 1999.

Colony, John J. III (Chick). Interview with the author. April 12, 1999.

Concord's Hurricane and Flood, September 21, 1938. Capital Offset Company. 1938.

Dalzell, Robert F. Jr. *Enterprising Elite: The Boston Associates and the World They Made*. Harvard University Press, 1987.

Dunwell, Steve. *The Run of the Mill*. David R. Godine, Publisher, Inc., 1978.

Eastman, Jeannie. "The Great New England Hurricane." *Common Threads, The Newsletter of Harrisville, New Hampshire,* August 1998.

Freak Winds. L. A. Cummings, 1938.

French, George, ed. *New England: What It Is and What It Is to Be.* Boston Chamber of Commerce, 1911.

Gordon, Robert B., and Patrick Malone. *The Texture of Industry: An Archaeological View of the Industrialization of North America.* Oxford University Press, 1994.

Gregory, Frances W. *Nathan Appleton: Merchant and Entrepreneur, 1779–1861*. University Press of Virginia, 1975.

Hanlan, James P. *The Working Population of Manchester, N.H., 1840–1886*. UMI Research Press, 1981.

Horwitz, Morton J. *The Transformation of American Law, 1780–1860*. Harvard University Press, 1977.

Humphrey, John. *Water Power of Nubanisit Lake and River, as used by Cheshire Mills, Harrisville N.H.* 1903.

Hunter, Louis C. *A History of Industrial Power in the United States, 1780–1930. Vol. One: Waterpower in the Century of the Steam Engine*. The University Press of Virginia, 1979.

Hutton, John. "Windthrow." *Appalachia*, June 15, 1972.

Jaher, Frederic Cople. *The Urban Establishment*. University of Illinois Press, 1982.

Johnson, John W., ed. *Historic U.S. Court Cases 1690–1990*. Garland Publishing, 1992.

Josephson, Hannah. *The Golden Threads*. 1949. Reprinted: Russell & Russell, 1967.

Kasson, John F. *Civilizing the Machine: Technology and Republican Values in America, 1776–1900*. Penguin Books, 1977.

Keene Evening Sentinel. Emergency Edition, September 24, 1938.

McCarthy, Joe. *Hurricane!* American Heritage Press, 1969.

McGouldrick, Paul F. *New England Textiles in the 19th Century: Profits and Investment*. Harvard University Press, 1968.

Minsinger, William Elliott. *The 1938 Hurricane*. Blue Hill Observatory, 1988.

Nashua Telegraph. *Hurricane: The Complete Historical Record of New England's Stricken Area, September 21, 1938*. Nashua Telegraph, 1938.

New Hampshire Department of Environmental Services, Water Division, Dam Safety Bureau. Lake Nubanusit Lake Level Hearings files.

The New York Times. "Hurricane." September 21, 1938.

Park, Edwards. "My Birthday Hurricane." *Yankee*, September 1998.

Readio, James Jr. "September 21, 1938." *Yankee*, September 1973.

Rousmaniere, James A. Jr. "The Hurricane of '38." *The Keene Sentinel*, September 17, 1988.

Sheets, Bob, and Jack Williams. *Hurricane Watch*. Vintage Books, 2001.

Steinberg, Theodore. *Nature Incorporated: Industrialization and the Waters of New England*. Cambridge University Press, 1991.

Stewart, John Q. "New England Hurricane." *Harper's Magazine*, January 1939.

Struthers, Parke Hardy. *Tellable Tales from Nelson, N.H.* Merriconn Press, 1955.

Temin, Peter, ed. *Engines of Enterprise: An Economic History of New England*. Harvard University Press, 2000.

Tharp, Louise Hall. *The Appletons of Beacon Hill*. Little, Brown and Co., 1973.

Thoreau, Henry David. *A Week on the Concord and Merrimack Rivers*. 1849. Reprinted, The Library of America, 1985.

Weare Junior Historical Society. *The Flood and Hurricane of 1938*. Weare Junior Historical Society, 1972.

Timescape: *"I Opened the Store as Usual."*

Antrim History Committee. *Parades and Promenades: Antrim, New Hampshire . . . the second hundred years*. Antrim History Committee, 1977.

The Antrim Reporter. "Class of 1900, A.H.S. A Promising Class of Twelve go out from Antrim High School." July 4, 1900.

——. "Daring Work. Antrim Post Office Entered. Geo. E. Colby's Horse Stolen." September 3, 1902.

——."A Successful Ending. Of the Popular Annual Gathering, Oak Park Fair, Greenfield." September 17, 1902.

Davis, Kermit L., ed. *Antrim, New Hampshire: Footnotes to History. From the Diaries of Clinton Preston Davis*. Vo1. 1,

1898–1901, Vol. 2, 1902–1906, Vol. 3, 1907–1913. "As transcribed and annotated by his son Kermit L. Davis." James A. Tuttle Library reference collection, Antrim, N.H. (1993, 1995, 1996.)

Mallon, Thomas. *A Book of One's Own: People and Their Diaries.* Ticknor & Fields, 1984.

The Peterborough Transcript. "Oak Park Fair." September 11, 1902.

Clarence Derby's USA

Derby, Charlie. Interview with author. October 13, 2003.

Derby, Clarence. "Goodnow & Derby, Pictures, Comments, Advertising." Volumes at Peterborough Public Library and Peterborough Historical Society, MMS 10. (Written 1989–1990.)

Peterborough Historical Society Archives. Derby's Department Store Collection, MSS 10.

Peterborough Historical Society, *Our Changing Town: Peterborough 1939–1989*. Peterborough Historical Society, 1996.

Underhill, Paco. *The Call of the Mall.* Simon and Schuster, 2004.

Timescape: *Pasture Day*

Friends of the Wapack Trail archives, Peterborough Town Library, Historical Room.

Hall, Constance A. Marion Davis interviews.

The Old Homestead

Allsop, Kenneth. *Hard Travellin': The Hobo and His History*. New American Library, 1967.

Avrich, Paul. *The Haymarket Tragedy*. Princeton University Press, 1984.

Bordman, Gerald. *American Theatre: A Chronicle of Comedy and Drama 1869-1914*. Oxford University Press, 1994.

——,ed. *The Oxford Companion to American Theatre*. Oxford University Press, 1984.

Brady, James Jay. *Life of Denman Thompson (Joshua Whitcomb)*. E. A. McFarland & Alex. Comstock, Publishers/Academy of Music, 1888.

Brock, H. I. "The Old Homestead Comes Home." *The New York Times*, August 13, 1933.

Brown, Thomas Allston. *A History of the New York Stage from the First Performance in 1732 to 1901*. Dodd, Mead and Co. 1903.

Bruce, Robert V. *1877: Year of Violence*. Quadrangle Books, 1970.

Current Literature. "The Old Homestead—The Greatest Popular Success of the American Stage." December 1908.

——. "The Significance of Joshua Whitcomb." June 1911.

Demarest, David P., ed. *"The River Ran Red": Homestead 1892*. University of Pittsburgh Press, 1992.

Derthick, Martha. *The National Guard in Politics*. Harvard University Press, 1965.

Foner, Philip F. *The Autobiographies of the Haymarket Martyrs*. Humanities Press, 1969.

——. *The Great Labor Uprising of 1877*. Monad Press, 1977.

Gelb, Arthur, and Barbara Gelb. *O'Neill: Life with Monte Cristo*. Applause Books, 2000.

Goldman, William. *The Season: A Candid Look at Broadway*. Harcourt, Brace & World, Inc., 1969.

Granger, Melvenah Thompson. Scrapbook. c. 1887–1892. Swanzey Historical Society.

Green, James. *Death in the Haymarket*. Pantheon Books, 2006.

Guillot, Ellen Elizabeth. *Social Factors in Crime As Explained by American Writers of the Civil War and Post Civil War Period*. Dissertation. Philadelphia, 1943.

Hanna, George R. *Denman Thompson and The Old Homestead*. Unpublished, 1939.

Harrison, Jonathan Baxter. "Certain Dangerous Tendencies in American Life." *The Atlantic Monthly*, October 1878.

Herron, Ima Honaker. *The Small Town in American Drama*. Southern Methodist University Press, 1969.

Hewitt, Barnard. *Theatre U.S.A. 1665 to 1957*. McGraw-Hill Book Co., Inc., 1959.

Higginson, Thomas Wentworth. "American Audiences." *The Atlantic*, January 1905.

Hornblow, Arthur. *A History of the Theatre in America*. 1919. Reprinted, Benjamin Blom, 1965.

Howells, William Dean. "Editor's Study." *Harper's New Monthly*, July 1889.

Hunnicutt, Benjamin Kline. *Work Without End: Abandoning Shorter Hours for the Right to Work*. Temple University Press, 1988.

Jamieson, Kathleen Hall. *Eloquence in an Electronic Age: The Transformation of Political Speechmaking*. Oxford University Press, 1988.

Jones, Howard Mumford. *The Age of Energy: Varieties of American Experience 1865-1915*. Viking Press, 1970.

Julian, John. *A Dictionary of Hymnology, Setting Forth the Origin and History of Christian Hymns of All Ages and Nations*. Vol. 1, 1907. Reprinted, Dover Publications, 1957.

Kazin, Alfred. *On Native Grounds*. Harcourt, Brace & Co., 1942.

Keller, Morton. *Affairs of State: Public Life in Late 19th-Century America*. Harvard University Press, 1977.

Krause, Paul. *The Battle for Homestead 1880–1892*. University of Pittsburgh Press, 1992.

Lears, T. J. Jackson. *No Place of Grace: Antimodernism and the Transformation of American Culture 1880–1920*. Pantheon Books, 1981.

Lewis, Philip C. *Trouping: How the Show Came to Town*. Harper & Row, 1973.

Levine, Lawrence W. *Highbrow/Lowbrow: The Emergence of Cultural Hierarchy in America*. Harvard University Press, 1988.

Leyda, Jay, and Charles Musser. *Before Hollywood: Turn-of-the-Century American Film*. Hudson Hills Press, 1987.

Licht, Walter. *Industrializing America: The Nineteenth Century*. Johns Hopkins University Press, 1995.

Lukas, J. Anthony. *Big Trouble*. Simon & Schuster, 1997.

Lutz, Tom. *American Nervousness, 1903*. Cornell University Press, 1991.

Mackay, Frederic E., and Charles E.L. Wingate, eds. *Famous American Actors of To-Day*. Thomas Y. Crowell & Co., 1896.

Magnus, Julian. "The Condition of the American Stage." *The North American Review*, February 1887.

Mammen, Edward William. *The Old Stock Company School of Acting: A Study of the Boston Museum*. Trustees of the [Boston] Public Library, 1945.

Matthews, Brander. "The Dramatic Outlook in America." *Harper's New Monthly*, May 1889.

May, Henry F. *The End of American Innocence*. Quadrangle Books, 1964.

Meserve, Walter J. *An Outline History of American Drama*. Littlefield, Adams & Co., 1965.

Miller, Douglas T. *The Birth of Modern America, 1820–1850*. Pegasus, 1970.

Monkkonen, Eric H., ed. *Walking to Work: Tramps in America, 1790–1935*. University of Nebraska Press, 1984.

Moody, Richard. *America Takes the Stage*. Indiana University Press, 1955.

Moses, Montrose J., and John Mason Brown, eds. *The American Theatre As Seen By Its Critics 1752–1934*. Cooper Square Publishers, Inc., 1967.

Musser, Charles. *Before the Nickelodeon: Edwin S. Porter and the Edison Manufacturing Company*. University of California Press, 1991.

The New York Times. "The Old Homestead." January 11, 1887.

Odell, George C. D. *Annals of the New York Stage*. Vols. 13–15. Columbia University Press, 1927–49.

Painter, Nell Irvin. *Standing at Armageddon: The United States 1877-1916*. W.W. Norton & Co., 1987.

Quinn, Arthur Hobson. *A History of the American Drama, from the Beginning to the Civil War*. F. S. Crofts & Co., 1943.

——. *A History of the American Drama, from the Civil War to the Present Day*. 1927, 1936. Revised, Appleton-Century-Crofts, Inc., 1955.

Roediger, David R., and Philip S. Foner. *Our Own Time: A History of American Labor and the Working Day*. Greenwood Press, 1989.

Ryan, Mary P. *Civic Wars: Democracy and Public Life in the American City During the Nineteenth Century*. University of California Press, 1997.

Sicherman, Barbara. "Paradox of Prudence: Mental Health in the Gilded Age." *Journal of American History,* March 1976.

Sper, Felix. *From Native Roots*. The Caxton Printers, Ltd., 1948.

Tarbell, Ida. *All in the Day's Work*. The MacMillan Co., 1939.

Thompson, Denman. *The Old Homestead*. Walter H. Baker Co., 1923.

Tompkins, Eugene, and Quincy Kilby. *The History of the Boston Theatre 1854-1901*. 1908. Reprinted, Benjamin Blom, 1969.

Walsh, William H. *Historical and Personal Reminiscences of Denman Thompson: The Grand Old Man of the Dramatic Profession.* H. E. Cutler, c. 1910.

Wilmeth, Don B., and Tice L. Miller, eds. *Cambridge Guide to American Theatre.* Cambridge University Press, 1993.

——, and Christopher Bigsby. *The Cambridge History of American Theatre.* Cambridge University Press, 1998.

Timescape: *False Witness*

City of Keene, City Report and Other Reports, 1924.

Four Centuries of King Philip's War

A Walking Tour of Downtown Turners Falls, Massachusetts. Great Falls Discovery Center, 1995.

Albers, Jan. *Hands on the Land: A Survey of the Vermont Landscape.* The MIT Press, 2000.

Axtell, James. *Beyond 1492.* Oxford University Press, 1992.

Bourne, Russell. *The Red King's Rebellion.* Atheneum, 1990.

Bruchac, Joseph. *Roots of Survival: Native American Storytelling and the Sacred.* Fulcrum Publishing, 1996.

Bruchac, Marge. "Indian Doctors in 19th-C. New England: A Collection of Historical Excerpts from Various Sources Including Town Histories, Basketry Books, Herbals, Manuscript Papers." Old Sturbridge Village. November 1988.

——. "The Indian Doctor Meets the Yankee Physician." Conference paper, Old Sturbridge Village, Teacher Workshop, November 2000.

——. "Schaghticoke and Points North: Wobanaki Resistance and Persistence." August 17, 2005, draft. http://1704.deerfield.history.museum.

——. "Thoughts on Indian Images, Names, and Respect." December, 1999. www.nativeweb.org.

——, and Peter Thomas. "Locating Wissatinnewag: John Pynchon's Influence on Pocumtuck Diplomacy." Working draft January 2005.

Cadran, Larry. *The Courage of Conviction: The Story of William Turner*. American University and College Press, 2002.

Calloway, Colin G. *The Abenaki*. Chelsea House Publishers, 1989.

——, ed. *After King Philip's War: Presence and Persistence in Indian New England*. University Press of New England, 1997.

——, ed. *Dawnland Encounters: Indians and Europeans in Northern New England*. University Press of New England, 1991.

——, ed. *New Worlds for All: Indians, Europeans, and the Remaking of Early America*. The Johns Hopkins University Press, 1997.

——, and Neal Salisbury, eds. *Reinterpreting New England Indians and the Colonial Experience*. Colonial Society of Massachusetts, 2003.

Carlson, Richard G., ed. *Rooted Like the Ash Trees: New England Indians and the Land*. Eagle Wing Press, Inc., 1987.

Church, Colonel Benjamin. *Diary of King Philip's War 1675–76*. The Pequot Press, 1975.

Cloues, Richard. "The Planning and Development of Turners Falls, Massachusetts, 1865–1872." History of American City Planning, History of Architecture, Cornell University, Fall 1974.

Clifford, James. *The Predicament of Culture*. Harvard University Press, 1988.

Coombs, Linda. "Holistic History: Including the Wampanoag in an Exhibit at Plimoth Plantation." www.plimoth.org

Crosby, Alfred W. *Ecological Imperialism: The Biological Expansion of Europe, 900–1900*. Cambridge University Press, 1986.

Diamond, Jared. *Guns, Germs and Steel.* W.W. Norton & Co., 1998.

Deloria, Barbara, et al., eds. *Spirit & Reason: The Vine Deloria, Jr. Reader*. Fulcrum Publishing, 1999.

Deloria, Vine Jr. *For This Land: Writings on Religion.* Routledge, 1999.

Drake, James D. *King Philip's War: Civil War in New England 1675–1676.* University of Massachusetts Press, 1999.

Fennelly, Catherine. *Life in an Old New England Country Village.* Thomas Y. Crowell Co., 1969.

Foster, Michael K., William Cowan, eds. *In Search of New England's Native Past: Selected Essays by Gordon Day.* University of Massachusetts Press, 1998.

Gallagher, Nancy L. *Breeding Better Vermonters.* University Press of New England, 1999.

Grace, Catherine O'Neill, and Margaret M. Bruchac. *1621: A New Look at Thanksgiving.* National Geographic Society, 2001.

Heath, Dwight, ed. *Mourt's Relation: A Journal of the Pilgrims at Plymouth.* 1622. Reprinted, Applewood Books, 1986.

Josephy, Alvin M., Jr. *America in 1492.* Alfred A. Knopf, 1992.

Kostyk, Dennis, and David Westphal, producers. *Wabanaki: A New Dawn.* Video. Maine Indian Tribal State Commission, 1995.

Grinde, Donald A., and Bruce E. Johansen. *Ecocide of Native America.* Clear Light Publishers, 1995.

Grumet, Robert S. *Historic Contact: Indian People and the Colonists in Today's Northeastern U.S. in the Sixteenth through Eighteenth Century.* University of Oklahoma Press, 1995.

——, ed. *Northeastern Indian Lives, 1632-1816.* The University of Massachusetts Press, 1996.

Larkin, Jack. *The Reshaping of Everyday Life, 1790-1840.* Harper & Row, Publishers, 1988.

Lepore, Jill. *The Name of War: King Philip's War and the Origins of American Identity*. Alfred A. Knopf, 1998.

Lincoln, Charles H. *Narratives of the Indian Wars 1675–1699*. 1913. Reprinted: Barnes & Noble, 1959.

Main, Jackson Turner. "The Distribution of Property in Colonial Connecticut" in *The Human Dimensions of Nation Making*. James Kirby Martin, ed. The State Historical Society of Wisconsin, 1976.

Mansfield, Howard. "I Still Live." *Yankee*, November 2001.

Martin, Calvin, ed. *The American Indian and the Problem of History*. Oxford University Press, 1987.

McBride, Bunny. *Women of the Dawn*. University of Nebraska Press, 1999.

McCallum, Kent. *Old Sturbridge Village*. Harry M. Abrams, Inc., 1996.

McPhee, John. "A Selective Advantage." *The New Yorker*, September 11, 2000.

Miller, Peter S. and Kyle J. Scott. *Montague: Images of America*. Arcadia Publishing, 2000.

Montague Reporter. "Turners Falls [High School] Indians." Editorial. January 8, 2004.

Montgomery, David R. *King of Fish: The Thousand-Year Run of Salmon*. Westview Press, 2003.

Montgomery, Sy. *Spell of the Tiger: The Man-Eaters of the Sunderbans*. Houghton Mifflin, 1995.

O'Connell, Barry, ed. *On Our Own Ground: The Complete Writings of William Apess, A Pequot*. The University of Massachusetts Press, 1992.

Pressey, Edward Pearson. *History of Montague: A Typical Puritan Town*. 1910. Reprinted: The Montague Historical Society, Inc., 1987.

Pritzker, Barry M. *Native America Today*. ABC-CLIO, 1999.

Radhakrishnan, Sarvepalli, and Charles A. Moore, eds. *A Sourcebook in Indian Philosophy*. Princeton University Press, 1957.

Salisbury, Neal. *Manitou and Providence: Indians, Europeans, and the Making of New England, 1500–1643*. Oxford University Press, 1982.

——, ed. *The Sovereignty and Goodness of God: Together with the Faithfulness of His Promises Displayed: Being a Narrative of the Captivity and Restoration of Mary Rowlandson and Related Documents*. Bedford/St. Martin's, 1997.

Schultz, Eric B., and Michael J. Tougias. *King Philip's War*. The Countryman Press, 1999.

Silko, Leslie Marmon. *Yellow Woman and a Beauty of Spirit: Essays on Native American Life Today*. Simon and Schuster, 1996.

Slotkin, Richard, and James K. Folsom, eds. *So Dreadfull a Judgment: Puritan Responses to King Philip's War 1676–1677*. Wesleyan University Press, 1978.

Small Wars Center of Excellence, U.S. Marine Corps. http://smallwars.quantico.usmc.mil/sw_past.asp.

Speck, Frank G. "Reflections Upon the Past and Present of the Massachusetts Indians." *Bulletin of the Massachusetts Archaeological Society*, Vol. 4, No. 3, April 1943.

Town of Montague, Massachusetts. *1754–1954: Historical Review and Complete Celebration Program*. Montague Bicentennial Celebration, 1954.

Webb, Stephen Saunders. *1676: The End of American Independence*. Alfred A. Knopf, 1984.

Wilkins, W. J. *Hindu Mythology*. 1882. Reprinted: Rupa & Co., Calcutta, 1992.

Wilson, James. *The Earth Shall Weep: A History of Native America*. Atlantic Monthly Press, 1999.

Wiseman, Frederick Matthew. "'A Real Hatchet Job': Erasing Ethnic History in the Green Mountain State." Revision of a paper presented at the Northeastern Anthropological Association, March 23, 2003.

——. *The Voice of the Dawn: An Autohistory of the Abenaki Nation*. University Press of New England, 2001.

Zimmer, Heinrich. *Philosophies of India*. Princeton University Press, 1951.

Acknowledgments

For taking the time to be interviewed or to review parts of this book I thank Marge Bruchac, John (Chick) Colony III, Kermit L. Davis, Charlie and Ellen Derby, Jerome Ebbinghausen, and Bob Rodat.

For research help, I thank Michelle Stahl, executive director of the Peterborough Historical Society; Patricia G. Hoffman, New Ipswich Historical Society; Alan Rumrill, executive director of the Historical Society of Cheshire County; Swanzey Historical Museum; the fine librarians at the Peterborough Town Library, and the James A. Tuttle Library, Antrim; Jim Rousmaniere; Constance A. Hall; and Hancock Library Director Amy Markus for her tireless work in the trenches of Interlibrary Loan.

Parts of three chapters have previously appeared in a different form, in the anthology *Where the Mountain Stands Alone: Stories of Place in the Monadnock Region*. My thanks to John Harris, direcor of the Monadnock Institute of Nature, Place and Culture, and to Mortimer Peebles for their help. And thanks to Lida Stinchfield for proofing.

Once again my deepest thanks to my agent Christina Ward, and to my wife and editor, Sy Montgomery.